Documenting discrimination against migrant workers in the labour market

A comparative study of four European countries

Documenting discrimination against migrant workers in the labour market

A comparative study of four European countries

Edited by
Roger Zegers de Beijl

INTERNATIONAL LABOUR OFFICE · GENEVA

Zegers de Beijl, R. (ed.)

Documenting discrimination against migrant workers in the labour market: A comparative study of four European countries

Geneva, International Labour Office, 2000

Racial discrimination/,/Recruitment/,/Equal employment opportunity/,/migrant worker/,/ethnic group/,/comparison/,/Belgium/,/Germany/,/Netherlands/,/Spain/. 04.02.7

ISBN 92-2-111387-6

ILO Cataloguing-in-Publication Data

Printed in Great Britain by The Cromwell Press, Trowbridge, Wiltshire

PREFACE

In the early 1990s, the International Migration Branch of the International Labour Organization (ILO) embarked on a research project to combat discrimination against (im)migrants and ethnic minorities in the world of work in a number of countries in North America and western Europe. The overall investigation included four main phases: (1) documenting the occurrence of unlawful discrimination in access to employment; (2) assessing the scope and efficacy of existing anti-discrimination legislation; (3) demonstrating how voluntary measures can enhance the progress made by comprehensive and stringent legal measures; and (4) organizing national and international seminars to discuss policies aimed at reducing discrimination within individual enterprises.

This study documents the occurrence of unlawful discrimination at the point of access to employment in four countries of the European Union (EU). For this purpose, the situation testing methodology used is described and its pros and cons are assessed in relation to other approaches. Then, its application and findings in Belgium, Germany, the Netherlands and Spain are explained. Finally, a cross-country analysis of these conclusions reveals what lessons can be drawn and subsequently applied by other countries seeking to fight this kind of discrimination.

A draft version of this publication was distributed to those present at the ILO Tripartite High-Level Meeting on Achieving Equality in Employment for Migrant Workers, which convened in Geneva, Switzerland, from 8 to 11 March 2000, to examine the findings and implications of the ILO research project. A framework and inventory of measures and mechanisms to combat discrimination and promote equal opportunity were developed at the meeting, as were best practices and a set of recommendations for follow-up activities. The ILO was called on to continue acting as a catalyst for the promotion of better access to employment for migrant and ethnic minority workers and for the assessment of the impact of initiatives at the levels of enterprises, workers' and employers' organizations, and local and national governments.

The study's findings on the occurrence of discrimination against migrant and ethnic minority job applicants in the four countries analysed are disturbing, and reveal the enormity of the challenge facing the international community in general and the ILO in particular. The situation testing methodology revealed the total net discrimination rates after all three stages of the application procedure had been completed to be 33 per cent in Belgium, 37 per cent in the Netherlands and 36 per cent in Spain respectively. In other words, in these three countries more than one-third of the tested vacancies for semi-skilled jobs were closed to young, male applicants of migrant and ethnic minority origin. In Germany, it proved impossible to carry out the final stage of the application process. After the first two stages, the cumulative net discrimination rate was found to be 19 per cent, which is considerably lower than the results of the other three countries at this point; it is the same as in Belgium after completion of the first stage but lower than the scores gleaned from the first stages in the Netherlands and Spain.

This book had almost been completed when its editor, Roger Zegers de Beijl, died at the end of July 1999. The development and success of this ILO programme is a tribute to his vision, commitment and tenacious perseverance, but his greatest achievement lies in his having greatly increased awareness of discrimination in the industrialized migrant-receiving countries. A "turning point" has been reached, and most countries covered by the ILO project are now taking decisive steps to reach true equality in employment.

Manolo Abella
Chief
International Migration Branch
International Labour Organization

CONTENTS

Figures

Tables

INTRODUCTION

Roger Zegers de Beijl[1]

Since the end of the Second World War the phenomenon of migration on an international scale has been on the increase. The reasons for this trend include the growing internationalization of the world economy, the convergence of the world's communication and media systems, the ever-widening gap between rich and poor countries, rapid population growth, the destruction of the environment, armed conflicts and the continuing prevalence of oppression. These factors have led many people from poorer countries to look for income-earning opportunities or safe havens in richer countries.

The worldwide population of migrant workers, who are defined as people who are economically active in a country of which they are not nationals but excluding asylum seekers and refugees, is estimated by the ILO to be between 36 and 42 million. If dependents are added to this estimate, the total population of migrants stands at between 80 to 97 million. Europe is the region with the highest concentration of non-nationals in the world, with between 26 and 30 million people who are non-national residents.[2]

Recent migration trends in Europe

Migration patterns have long shaped the demographic structure of Europe. In the aftermath of the Second World War, immigration from the countries of southern and eastern Europe played a large part in reconstructing the economies of western Europe (Groenendijk and Hampsink, 1995), while at the same time large numbers of refugees and displaced people also moved into the area. As a result, for the first time in its history western Europe became a region of net immigration. In the 1950s and 1960s, the rapidly expanding economies of France, Germany and the United Kingdom attracted large numbers of migrant workers from the countries of southern Europe as well as from the former Socialist Federal Republic of Yugoslavia and North Africa (Stalker,

1

1997). These workers were warmly welcomed, since they took up employment in areas that the native populations found unattractive – because of low pay or poor working conditions, for example. However, the sudden rise in domestic unemployment levels as a result of the oil crisis of the early 1970s changed people's attitudes to migrants. General restrictions on immigration flows were imposed in most western European countries – restrictions that have, with few exceptions, such as for highly skilled professionals, remained in place ever since. Interestingly, the newly imposed restrictions did not have their intended effect of immediately stemming migration levels:

Predictably ... most migrants who were welcomed in the sixties chose not to give up their residence privileges as a result of the rising unemployment, mindful of the fact that the general ban on immigration would have prevented them from re-entering ... at a future date. Furthermore ... a number of these migrants reunited their families. At the same time, refugees from the Iran-Iraq war, as well as from other conflict situations, began arriving ... as asylum seekers.[3]

As a consequence of this chain migration, the numbers of non-nationals in Europe increased rather than decreased immediately after the ban was imposed, although by the beginning of the 1980s the influx of family members had slowed down. With the immigration ban still in place, many people who would previously have been permitted entry now began looking for alternative ways of getting into Europe, through temporary migration schemes and contract migration as well as clandestinely and by claiming asylum. While Poland and the former Socialist Federal Republic of Yugoslavia remained the main countries of origin, many of these newer migrants now came from further afield – from northern Africa, Asia and Latin America (Groenendijk and Hampsink, 1995). Despite the official ban on labour immigration, demand for a cheap, docile labour force persisted. As a result, most of the newer migrants managed to find work and many have remained in the region permanently. Table I.1 summarizes the evolution of migration to western Europe from 1950 to 1990.[4]

Migrants and the labour markets of western Europe

On arriving in western Europe, many migrants worked for lower wages and in poorer conditions than native workers, for most of them naturally aspired "to a better future for their children and grandchildren" (Bovenkerk, 1992, p. 1). Despite high labour force participation rates in all European countries, however, migrant and migrant-descended populations are disproportionately represented among the ranks of the long-term unemployed. When they are employed, they tend to be disproportionately employed and concentrated in the

Table I.1   Foreign resident population in western Europe, 1950–1990
(in thousands and by percentage of total population)

Country	1950		1970		1982*		1990	
	No.	%	No.	%	No.	%	No.	%
Austria	323	4.7	212	2.8	203	4.0	512	6.6
Belgium	368	4.3	696	7.2	886	9.0	905	9.1
Denmark	–	–	–	–	–	2.0	161	3.1
Finland	11	0.3	6	0.1	12	0.3	35	0.9
France	1 765	4.1	2 621	5.3	3 680	6.8	3 608	6.4
Germany (FRD)	568	1.1	2 977	4.9	4 667	7.6	5 242	8.2
Greece	31	0.4	93	1.1	60	0.7	70	0.9
Ireland	–	–	–	–	69	2.0	90	2.5
Italy	47	0.1	–	–	312	0.5	781	1.4
Liechtenstein	3	19.6	7	36.0	9	36.1	–	–
Luxembourg	29	9.9	63	18.4	96	26.4	109	28.0
Netherlands	104	1.1	255	2.0	547	3.9	692	4.6
Norway	16	0.5	–	–	91	2.2	143	3.4
Portugal	21	0.3	–	–	64	0.6	108	1.0
Spain	93	0.3	291	0.9	418	1.1	415	1.1
Sweden	124	1.8	411	1.8	406	4.9	484	5.6
Switzerland	285	6.1	1 080	17.2	926	14.7	1 100	16.3
United Kingdom	–	–	–	–	2 137	3.9	1 875	3.3
Total	5 100	1.3	10 200	2.2	15 000	3.1	16 600	4.5

- = missing data.

* 1982 was chosen as the data year for the 1980s as data for this year is more complete than for 1980. The totals include interpolated figures for any missing data.

Source: Fassner and Munz (1992).

type of poorly paid and insecure jobs that the national population prefers not to do. This labour market marginalization has serious consequences, which have already been well-documented, for the social integration of migrants:

The theory of multiple and cumulative causation explains how a denial of equal opportunities in various fields produces a group of people unable to attach themselves to the mainstream of society. Rejection in the labour market results in restriction of possibilities of finding suitable housing and this in turn results in relocation in neighbourhoods where children encounter fewer chances to follow good education. Poor education makes for fewer chances in the labour market and so on. Rejected individuals may respond by lowering their efforts for social advancement or by turning away from an unjust system. Rejected groups may find themselves suffering from a multitude of social problems (poverty, crime, substance abuse, etc.) that make it hard to escape from this vicious circle.[5]

The social and labour market marginalization of migrants can be explained by the interplay of a number of supply- and demand-side factors. Recently arrived migrants, it is argued, tend to be low-skilled, have a poor command of the language of the host country and have fewer qualifications than the national population. And, if we take into consideration the fact that the authorities of a country seldom regard qualifications obtained abroad as highly as those gained in their own education system, it is then easy to see that recently arrived migrant workers can be at a great disadvantage in the labour market.

In response to this, the integration policies of many western European countries have focused on reducing these supply-side disadvantages by encouraging migrants to complete their education and to take language and vocational training courses. Courses that familiarize migrants with the culture and institutions of the host country can help ensure that a newly arrived migrant makes a smooth transition within the country of employment. However, these kinds of policies do not address the problems faced by long-term migrants and ethnic minorities.

The predicament of settled migrants and ethnic minorities in the labour market is remarkably similar to that of newly arrived migrants, but is less readily explained by supply-side variables. Long-term or permanently settled migrants, naturalized citizens and members of ethnic minorities born in European and North American countries have few of the difficulties of recent immigrants: they tend to speak the national language fluently (in many cases as a first language) and may have been educated in the host country. Moreover, in many countries members of certain ethnic minority groups are more likely than nationals to complete secondary and tertiary education. Yet, these groups continue to be over-represented among the ranks of the unemployed and disproportionately employed and so are becoming increasingly marginalized from society. This indicates that demand-side factors may be playing a significant role in dictating the labour market opportunities open to migrant and ethnic minority workers. One of these factors is, potentially at least, discrimination.

Why discrimination is a problem

There are several reasons why policy-makers, legislators, employers, consumers, non-governmental organizations (NGOs), trade unions and service
providers should tackle the problem of discrimination. In particular, the moral,
social and economic arguments need to be considered.

Moral considerations

The moral argument for non-discrimination carries a great deal of weight in both
the international and national domains. It stems from the basic human rights
premise that all human beings are equal and deserve to be treated as such. Such
principles are embedded in the United Nations (UN) Charter, the Universal
Declaration of Human Rights and the ILO Declaration of Philadelphia, as well
as in the 1998 ILO Declaration on Fundamental Principles and Rights at Work –
all documents that have been virtually universally accepted. Determined to outlaw
discriminatory practices, many states have agreed to a variety of legally binding
human rights instruments and international labour standards against various forms
of discrimination. The moral reasons for treating all individuals equally often
appear to be intuitive and are regularly cited by politicians as justifying specific
policies or the signing of human rights instruments.[6]

Social considerations

The social argument against discrimination is that society disintegrates under discrimination. Race riots, race-related arson attacks, racially motivated murders and
the proliferation of neo-Nazi and skinhead organizations are all manifestations of
the socially detrimental consequences of leaving discrimination unchecked.
Equally, violent backlashes against inequality are also more likely to occur when
discrimination is not addressed.[7] With considerable numbers of non-nationals and
members of ethnic minorities living permanently and legally in migrant-receiving
countries, governments that are reluctant to implement effective anti-discrimination measures as an essential part of wider integration policies and employers who
are unwilling to acknowledge their corporate responsibility as members of a
civilized society may inadvertently be contributing to the disintegration of society.[8]

Economic considerations

Economically speaking, it is not only society but also the individual employer
who pays the costs of discrimination. By discriminating, employers are failing
to use the full potential of the human resources available to them and are,

therefore, neither maximizing production nor minimizing costs, which is contrary to all economic sense. By changing strategy and acting in a non-discriminatory manner, employers could avoid this unnecessary competitive disadvantage. A number of economically-based arguments against discrimination and in favour of equal treatment can be given.

By discriminating on irrelevant grounds, such as nationality and race, at the recruitment stage, employers are potentially passing over highly qualified candidates. Were recruitment carried out on the basis of aptitude alone, then the best possible workforce could be acquired. Similarly, it has also been shown that by allowing discrimination to occur in the workplace, the employer is encouraging the disruption of teamwork, higher rates of absenteeism and reducing morale and commitment. In addition, there is the possibility that bad publicity will be attracted, because of potential allegations of discrimination.[9] A diverse workforce, however, with a wide range of skills and experience is more likely to be creative and open to new ideas than one made up of a homogeneous group of people. A diverse workforce, therefore, adds value to business activities through increased creativity and better problem-solving capacities.

Migrants and ethnic minorities can also have a privileged insight into markets abroad, which is of particular value in the new globalized economy. They are likely to have contacts abroad and speak the language of client states. Harnessing these skills give employers who do not discriminate a competitive advantage over those that do. At the national level, migrants and ethnic minorities are members of increasingly large communities who wield considerable influence as consumers. Migrant and ethnic minority can provide information on marketing strategies aimed at these largely undeveloped markets. It is predicted that the migrant and ethnic minority populations in the countries studied by the ILO will expand considerably in the future and will, therefore, make up a highly significant proportion of the buying public. Furthermore, the employer of a multi-ethnic workforce, being more representative of the multi-ethnic society prevailing in many countries, is more likely to attract custom, talented job applicants and investors than the employer who discriminates. As more people realise that discrimination is morally and socially unacceptable, so it also becomes less economically viable to discriminate – consumers, employees and investors are beginning to value fair-mindedness and are rewarding this behaviour when they see it within companies.

The ILO research project

At the beginning of the 1990s, the International Migration Branch of the ILO launched a project entitled "Combating discrimination against (im)migrants and ethnic minorities in the world of work" to shed light on the nature, extent and consequences of discrimination against migrant workers and to propose concrete measures that could be taken to combat it. More specifically, the project hopes to reduce levels of discrimination against regular-entry, long-stay migrant workers and ethnic minorities by informing policy-makers, employers, workers, NGOs and individuals engaged in anti-discrimination training how existing legislative measures and training activities can be made more effective. The project's aims can be broken down into four phases:

- To document the occurrence of unlawful discrimination in access to employment.
- To assess the scope and efficacy of existing anti-discrimination legislation and of specific measures for combating discrimination against migrant workers.
- To demonstrate how voluntary measures can reinforce and enhance the progress made by comprehensive and stringently enforced legal measures by making inventories and evaluations of training and education currently used to encourage equal opportunity and discourage non-discriminatory behaviour, in particular by analysing the training materials used in these programmes and the effects they have on trainees.
- To organize national and international seminars to involve ILO Constituents, policy-makers, individual employers, trade unions, personnel and line managers, personnel selectors, staff of employment agencies and representatives of their respective organizations, NGOs and migrant workers' organizations. The aims of the seminars are to discuss what changes may need to be made to existing legislation at the national level and to discuss policies aimed at combating discrimination at the enterprise level.

This study reports on the results of the first phase of the project. It explains how and why the particular testing methodology was developed and examines the individual findings of the participating countries: Belgium, Germany, the Netherlands and Spain. It also presents a cross-country analysis and, on the basis of some of the findings of the second and third phases of the project, offers proposals for tackling discrimination in the future.

Organization of the study

In order to calculate the incidence of discrimination against migrants and ethnic minorities in access to employment, it was decided to test the success rates of migrants at each level of the recruitment process in a number of application procedures for different sorts of jobs comprising a cross-section of the national labour market. To do this, a valid methodology had to be developed, one that suited the prevailing circumstances in each of the four countries under examination.

In Chapter 1, Frank Bovenkerk describes the ILO research methodology. He starts with an outline of the general strengths and weaknesses of the methodology in relation to other approaches and explains how the methodology has been developed in a number of countries over the years. He then gives a detailed description of the ILO design. This includes a discussion of the variables involved in a study of this nature and the limits imposed by the scope of the study. He describes how the testers were selected and trained, the testing process itself and the ethical issues involved. Methodologically sound research such as this is vital, for it determines just what is fact and what is fiction when it comes to establishing discrimination in the hiring process.

Chapters 2 to 5 describe how the research methodology was put into practice in Belgium, Germany, the Netherlands and Spain and presents the findings for each country. In Chapter 2 Bernadette Smeesters, Peter Arrijn, Serge Feld and André Nayer show the level of discrimination facing workers of migrant origin in Belgium. It demonstrates for the first time that male migrant workers face considerable discrimination when trying to gain access to the labour market, despite legislative measures prohibiting such practices. Chapter 3, by Andreas Goldberg and Dora Mourinho, presents the research findings of the situation in Germany, which also show the presence of discrimination in the labour market, despite the existence of anti-discrimination legislation. In Chapter 4, Frank Bovenkerk, Mitzi Gras and D. Ramsoedh show that even greater levels of discrimination confront migrants and ethnic minorities in the Netherlands. Miguel Angel de Prada, Walter Actis and Carlos Pereda reveal that discrimination against migrant workers is also widespread and on a large scale in Spain in Chapter 5.

Chapter 6 brings together the findings of the four country studies and shows by means of cross-country comparison where discrimination is most likely to occur in terms of the size of the establishment and the nature of the work being undertaken.

By evaluating the initiatives taken by a number of European countries, Chapter 7 suggests how policies and measures aimed at combating discrimination can be made more effective. This chapter draws on some of the findings of the second and third phases of the ILO project and argues that legislation alone is not enough to combat the levels of discrimination that migrants and ethnic minorities are confronting on a daily basis.

A note on terminology

The terminology used to describe the non-national population and descendants of non-nationals varies widely across the countries that were studied during this ILO project, reflecting the different political and social attitudes towards migrant groups. As Hoffmann-Nowotny has observed:

It is the very paradox of European migrations today that millions of people are living in foreign countries but are not designated as immigrants; neither do these countries see themselves as immigration countries. And vice versa, very few of the countries that send millions of their citizens to work abroad consider themselves as emigration countries in the narrow sense of the term. The concept of immigrant is paraphrased and terms such as "foreign worker", "guest worker", "foreign employee" or "migrant worker" are used.[10]

Migrant workers and ethnic minorities

The first discrepancy among the country studies is the use of terms relating to the target group of the ILO project – migrant workers. The problem is best illustrated by a few examples. In the United States, the term "immigrants" is taken to mean foreign-born American citizens, while a "nonimmigrant" is "an alien who seeks to enters the United States temporarily for a specific purpose and whose length of stay can range from a few days to five or more years".[11] In Germany, the term *Gastarbeiter* (guest worker) was introduced in the 1960s to refer to the non-nationals entering the country for specific purposes and who intended to stay there for a limited period only. In Denmark, the terms "migrant" and "ethnic minority" are used interchangeably to refer to any individual who is from a visibly different ethnic or national group, regardless of nationality. Finally, distinctions are also made in many European countries between first- and second-generation migrants, the former having moved to the country from their place of origin, the latter being their offspring, who may or may not hold nationality of the host state.

For reasons of consistency, the ILO project uses the terms "migrant" and "ethnic minority" according to the definitions given in the ILO Conventions and Recommendations. Thus, a migrant worker is a "person who migrates from one country to another with a view to being employed otherwise than on his [or her] own account".[12] This definition is broad enough to cover irregular-entry and stay migrants as well as those who enter and reside in the country with the authorization of the state.

The term "ethnic minority" is used in the project to refer to a migrant (or offspring of a migrant) who has been granted the nationality of the state through birth or naturalization. In most European countries, many ethnic minorities are also of visibly different ethnic origin, although this is, of course, not always necessarily the case.[13] As a result of their different features, ethnic minorities are often taken to be foreigners, despite the fact that they might hold the nationality of the state in question, so that they often face many of the same prejudices and discrimination as migrant workers.

9

The term "national" is used throughout this study to refer to the control group, that is, the group with which the opportunities of the reference or migrant group ethnic minority are compared. In places, the term "majority" is also used to refer to the control group and "minority" is used for the reference group. For the purposes of this ILO project, only discrimination against regular-entry and stay migrants and ethnic minorities was studied, given that equality of treatment and occupation of regular-entry migrants with national workers is one of the basic tenets of the ILO's protection of migrant workers.

Discrimination

The ILO Discrimination (Employment and Occupation) Convention, 1958 (No. 111) defines discrimination as any "distinction, exclusion or preference ... which has the effect of nullifying or impairing equality of opportunity or treatment in employment or occupation as may be determined". In this Convention, the grounds for non-discrimination include race, colour, sex, religion, political opinion, national extraction or social origin. Convention No. 111 does not, however, prohibit discrimination on the grounds of nationality – the one characteristic that differentiates migrants from other members of society. It has been made clear by the ILO's Committee of Experts on the Application of Conventions and Recommendations that the concept of national extraction in the 1958 instrument does not refer to those distinctions that may be made between the citizens of one country and those of another, but to distinctions between citizens of the same country on the basis of a person's place of birth, ancestry or foreign origin (ILO 1996). Indeed, at a preliminary stage of the 1958 Convention, it was proposed to include nationality among the grounds for non-discrimination, but this was rejected, as were subsequent amendments to the same effect.

For the purposes of this project, discrimination can be said to have occurred when distinctions, exclusions or preferences are made between workers on the basis of their real or perceived nationality. As already stated, ethnic minorities who are nationals of the state in question often face discrimination on the grounds of their perceived nationality. It should also be mentioned that when establishing direct discrimination, it is the manifestation of the action and not the intention that needs to be verified. In other words, it is the result, and not the motivation behind the act that needs to be established.

A note on gender

In designing the project it was borne in mind that male and female migrants might be facing different kinds of discrimination and that, as a result of gender preferences, migrant women might be doubly discriminated against. It could not be assumed that women and men were interchangeable for the purposes of documenting the extent and nature of discrimination. However, doubling the resources and the scope of the project was not feasible, so it was decided to limit the project to documenting discrimination against just one of the sexes. Since it is largely men who have, up to now, migrated to Europe to find work, and since they regularly compete with nationals for jobs in a narrow concentration of sectors, it was decided to restrict the project to male workers. In some cases, such as in the Netherlands, limited studies used all-women teams, but this was not carried out on a wide-enough scale for any general conclusions to be drawn. The project was, and this book, therefore, is limited to documenting discrimination against male migrant workers. The recommendations for improving the efficacy of anti-discrimination legislation and training, as featured in the final chapter of this book, may, of course, be of more general application and it is hoped that the methodology developed by ILO will be used to document discrimination against women migrants in the future.

Notes

[1] This chapter is based on previous written work by ILO Migration Specialist, Roger Zegers de Beijl. In 1989 Zegers de Beijl joined the International Migration Branch of the ILO, where he developed the Office's work on discrimination against migrant workers. He died in 1999 shortly before completion of this book.

[2] These estimates are based on the ILO (1997).

[3] Hansen and McClure (1998), p. 1.

[4] Table taken from Stalker (1994), p. 190, of which the source is Fassman and Münz (1992).

[5] Bovenkerk (1992), p. 2.

[6] See Dex (1992), p. 6, for examples of political citations on the unjustness of discrimination. For a further discussion of the moral argument against discrimination, see Banton (1994), pp. 2–3 and Edwards (1995).

[7] For concrete examples of social unrest resulting from discrimination, see Wrench (1997b), pp. 33–36.

[8] On the issue of corporate responsibility in relation to migrant and ethnic minority workers, see Lindburg (1998), p. 5.

[9] See Wrench (1997b), p. vi and p. 36. For statistics on how much racial harassment and discrimination in the workplace costs employers in the United Kingdom, see the Commission for Racial Equality (CRE), 1995, pp. 11–13.

[10] Hoffmann-Nowotny (1976), quoted in Rist (1978), p. 3.

[11] United States General Accounting Office (GAO), 1992, p. 13.

[12] See Article 11 of the ILO Migration for Employment Convention (Revised), 1949 (No. 97) and the ILO Migrant Workers (Supplementary Provisions) Convention, 1975 (No. 143).

[13] Migrants who have no visibly different features include the white Irish in the United Kingdom and white eastern European migrants in western Europe.

THE RESEARCH METHODOLOGY   1

Frank Bovenkerk[1]

"Situation testing" is a research methodology that has been used to bring to light discrimination in many areas of life, and not just in work-related fields. In the Anglo-Saxon world, where the term is often used interchangeably with "audit testing", this methodology has been used to study the way in which people belonging to ethnic or racial[2] minorities are admitted to hotels, banks, bars, discos and other service establishments, as a means of assessing discrimination levels. Situation testing not only serves to make the problem of discrimination visible, it can also be used to monitor the effectiveness of legal measures and assess the degree of compliance with the law. Its findings have been used as evidence in individual lawsuits in the United States, although in other countries such evidence is not permissible in a court of law. It is a social science method that has been employed by governmental institutions, official or semi-official law enforcement agencies and NGOs.

Before the situation testing methodology developed for the ILO project is presented in detail, some basic distinctions between situation testing and the other methods commonly used to measure discrimination are outlined. In this way the strengths and limitations of the method as a means of measuring discrimination can be established and its suitability for the ILO project confirmed. A brief overview of the development of the method from an international perspective is also given.

Situation testing and other methods of measuring discrimination

In general, discrimination studies focus either on the *outcome* of discrimination or on the discrimination *process* itself. In the former case, this involves studying statistical data on the socio-economic position of migrants and ethnic minorities, their participation in the workforce, their representation in higher levels of jobs, their share in lay-offs and their income levels in relation to majority employees. When found, evidence of statistical imbalances can be interpreted as providing prima facie evidence of discrimination. This may result from direct and overt discrimination, but more often disparities are believed to result from the adverse impact of indirect or institutional discrimination. Regression analysis is often used to identify the relative importance of other variables. This approach to the study of discrimination has, however, several disadvantages. In particular, it presents no conclusive proof of discrimination as long as all the relevant variables have not been identified.

Situation testing, on the other hand, focuses on the *process* of discrimination rather than on the *outcome*. It is one of several techniques that have been used to study the discrimination process, each of which has its own strengths and limitations.

Laboratory tests

Discrimination experiments have been conducted in various laboratory settings. Recruiters are usually made to act out hypothetical employment situations, where a choice has to be made between applicants differing in majority or minority status. Although this method has the enormous advantage that all conditions except the dependent variable under study can be controlled by the person carrying out the experiment, such experiments are often conducted under less than realistic conditions, making it difficult to reflect the reality an actual organization would face in similar circumstances.

Attitude surveys

Surveys on racial or ethnic prejudices constitute by far the most developed branch of research in this field. Employers or personnel managers are interviewed and they fill out innumerable tests to identify their stereotypes and prejudices. The technique has been infinitely refined, instruments have been validated and the method allows the study of variations within the observed population and also the correlation of a multitude of other variables. In some cases, questionnaires have been so carefully designed that the interviewee cannot guess what the desired answers should be. The major drawback of this method is that no definite conclusions can be drawn about what happens in reality. In some instances, employers have been shown to discriminate although they showed no prejudicial tendencies in their attitude surveys, while in other instances employers demonstrating discriminatory attitudes have been shown not to discriminate in practice. In other words, attitudes and behaviour don't necessarily correspond.

Observation

No research has, as yet, been carried out based on the direct observation of the entire hiring process nor of any other selection procedure in which discrimination may occur. But even if managers or personnel directors could be persuaded to have their procedures scrutinized on such a sensitive issue as discrimination, it is likely that they would change their usual behaviour as a result of their knowingly being observed. Although this approach is ideal in theory, results would surely be biased by the obtrusive nature of the observation.

Interviews with managers

Employers and personnel managers have often been questioned about their recruitment, promotion and firing practices in relation to discrimination. Many claim that they have no problems or otherwise stress the difficulty of finding suitably qualified people from minority groups to fill their vacancies. While this type of research methodology can be of interest in that it reveals awareness of the non-discrimination norm, it is, in fact, an open invitation for people to give what they consider to be socially desired responses. Nevertheless, there are examples where managers have been shown to be remarkably frank about biased practices and the stereotypes on which these have been based.[3] However, how can one be sure who is being honest and who isn't? Even if a respondent is open about practices that would be considered discriminatory, does it follow that the respondent's account is accurate? Besides their own feelings, what other influences are brought to bear on their decisions? Even when people admit to being biased, this doesn't automatically mean that their behaviour and attitudes will correspond. When self-report studies about hiring practices have been checked unobtrusively, major differences have often been found in the results.[4]

Victimization experiments

In the late 1950s, the white American novelist John Howard Griffin went around disguised as an African-American, and then described the discrimination he experienced in the United States in the book *Black like me* (1960). His experiences had a major impact on American public opinion, at a time when the white majority obviously found it easier to identify with "one of their own" encountering discrimination and blatant racism. In the 1980s, Günter Wallraff disguised himself as a Turk, and described his degrading experiences (*Ganz unten*, 1985) of what it was like living as a *Gastarbeiter* in the Federal

Republic of Germany. While both accounts make for provocative reading, they have been criticized for the fact that it took white members of the established white majority population to convince the public that racism and the exploitation of foreign manpower is wrong. Of course, blacks and Turks had for years been trying to tell the world this, but who had believed them? Technically, both authors acted as testers, that is, as stimulus individuals who studied the reactions provoked in real-life situations to their assumed identities. While they are highly convincing human-interest stories, the nature of their evidence is necessarily anecdotal and closely connected with their individual personalities and subjective in interpretation. Yet, from a methodological point of view, this research strategy is sound. Discrimination is unjustified difference in treatment, and for treatment to be established as inferior, an instance of reference is required for comparison. Griffin's and Wallraff's accounts are convincing, precisely because all their lives they had experienced what it was to be treated as a member of the societal majority.

Victim surveys

These surveys have often been used to highlight the existence of discrimination, to provide telling examples of how it works and to highlight the social and psychological consequences for those confronted by it. This type of research has often been instrumental in putting the problem of discrimination on the political agenda. Yet these studies suffer from the same flaws in terms of reliability as other crime victim surveys, because they combine concrete experiences, the feelings these experiences aroused and an interpretation of these feelings on the part the victim. Results of victim surveys cannot claim to be representative of the real extent of discrimination as some individuals may overestimate its extent and others underestimate it. Potential victims who are sensitive to antipathy and rejection may exaggerate insignificant occurrences of discrimination and thereby appear less than convincing to the very public they would like to influence.[5] Moreover, objective tests, in particular those carried out in the United Kingdom on white or majority behaviour, have systematically proven that victim surveys underestimate the extent of discrimination.

Situation testing

In contrast to the methods described above, situation testing is a technique that preserves the real-life quality of observations while avoiding the unsystematic and subjective quality of the account of the private player. The stimulus consists of two testers, one belonging to a majority group, the other to a minority group, who elicit a response from a decision-maker in a real-life situation. When applied to testing for discrimination in access to employment, the two testers are matched for all the criteria that should concern an employer recruiting personnel. They need to be of the same age, have a similar educational background and work experience but must be of a different racial or ethnic background. They either make a written application or apply for a job vacancy by telephone. If one tester is hired and the other is not, the difference can – assuming that all other variables have been controlled – in principle be attributed to their different backgrounds. This reasoning assumes that race or ethnic background should not be a relevant criterion for selecting personnel.[6] If discrimination in the labour market is present, this should become evident by the number of test results pointing in the same direction. Although this method of research has many advantages, it can only be used to answer certain types of questions: it only measures the outcome of a selection process and not the *workings* of the process itself, nor the *attitudes* of the decision-makers.

Strengths and limitations of situation testing in comparison with other methods

The comparative strengths and limitations of situation testing in relation to other methods used to measure discrimination are as follows:

- To a reasonably accurate degree, situation testing shows to what extent the disadvantages of racial or ethnic groups are a direct result of discrimination. The direct and unequivocal measurement leaves no room for other explanations. However, when trying to explain disadvantages at large, it is not possible to assess the relative significance of discrimination in relation to other factors. In that case, social policy research, using the regression analysis of large sets of survey data, would be more useful.
- Situation testing combines much of the power of the controlled experiment with the authenticity of a real-life situation. It is flexible, because the stimulus can be presented to the decision-maker under extremely realistic conditions. If one is interested in the effect of changes in one variable only, a fully controlled laboratory experiment may be more appropriate.
- Situation testing studies patterns of behaviour rather than sentiments or dispositions that are believed to be behind concrete acts. If one needs to find out what the public thinks or the variations over time and space as they relate to immigrant or ethnic minority groups, an attitude survey would probably be more suitable.

- Situation testing yields valid results, since it reveals what people actually do rather than what they believe or say they do. For a management's point of view, as when an internal policy change is required to stop discrimination, interviewing the relevant managers would provide additional information.

- Situation testing is objective and does not rely on uncertain interpretations or feelings that can prove difficult to evaluate. For victims' impressions of a situation and their subjective feelings, victim surveys are more appropriate.

All these considerations make situation testing the most satisfactory and objective research method for determining the prevalence of discrimination in any given situation. When discrimination is found to exist using this method, it can rarely be denied. Although the technique is somewhat complicated in practice, its principles can be readily understood. It is also sensitive, revealing otherwise concealed practices, which is particularly important in a world where discriminatory practices have become more subtle and harder to detect. Direct discrimination has been made unlawful in all the countries covered in this book, although it can often be masked by seemingly courteous treatment. The particular characteristics of situation testing has allowed the methodology to become a valuable tool in legal actions, public debate and, ultimately, in influencing public policy-making.

Previous situation testing research

Situation testing has been used to uncover discriminatory treatment in many fields other than employment, such as discrimination in housing, granting loans by banks, admittance to hotels, restaurants or discos, car hire and insurance as well as in many more areas in the public or semi-public domain. The methodology first came to prominence in 1967 in the United Kingdom, when the London-based Policy Studies Institute, then the research bureau for Political and Economic Planning (PEP), used the technique to determine the extent to which specific employers were discriminating against post-Second World War immigrant groups, such as West Indians and Hungarians.[7] A more refined research design was then developed by McIntosh and Smith (1974) to test the occurrence of discrimination in access to unskilled jobs. This test used correspondence as the means of testing and employed a random and much larger sample than the previous test. Correspondence testing was also used by Hubbock and Carter (1980) to determine the extent of discrimination in access to semi-skilled jobs in industry in Nottingham,[8] while Brown and Gay (1985) used the same techniques as McIntosh and Smith to carry out a further series of situation tests to determine the effects of anti-discrimination legislation. Finally, Esmail and Everington (1993) also used situation testing to test for discrimination in access to jobs in the medical profession.

The findings of successive situation tests in the United Kingdom paved the way for the adoption and subsequent strengthening of Britain's Race Relations Act, and the methods used by British researchers have influenced or been adopted by researchers in other countries. In the Netherlands, Bovenkerk and Breuning-van Leeuwen (1978) adopted McIntosh and Smith's methods to investigate possible discrimination against ethnic minority job applicants in Amsterdam. This was the first study to include gender as a variable and it also drew attention to the fact that discrimination tends to decrease as the skills level required for the job increases. Furthermore, the study revealed that discrimination levels tends to decrease in areas where there are labour shortages.[9] Situation tests were used again in the Netherlands by Den Uyl et al. (1986) and Meloen (1991) to demonstrate the willingness of temporary employment agencies to comply with discriminatory requests by employers. The results of the first study led to the implementation of a code of practice by the country's Confederation of Commercial Employment Agencies (ABU); the second study showed that 90 per cent of agencies were willing to break the law even after the code had been adopted.

Although situation tests have been used in other European countries,[10] it is in the Anglo-Saxon world that the methodology has been applied most extensively. In Canada, Henry and Ginzberg (1985) used both in-person and telephone situation testing to demonstrate considerable levels of discrimination against educated applicants of African, West Indian and Indo-Pakistani origin in the 18–25 age group when applying for jobs.[11] In Australia, Riach and Rich (1992) used correspondence situation testing over a four-year period to provide evidence of discrimination against job applicants of Greek and Vietnamese origin in the Melbourne area.[12] But by far the greatest amount of situation testing research has been carried out in the United States, where it is known as "audit testing" or "auditing". It has been used since the late 1960s in the enforcement of fair housing laws, and the evidence from these tests has been admitted in the courts to prove racial discrimination by rental agents and landlords. The first audit test on the labour market in the United States was carried out by Newman (1978) to check whether affirmative action programmes were working in practice. Newman's research, interestingly, varied the credentials of black and white applicants.[13]

The Urban Institute (UI) in Washington, DC was the first body to commission the development of a general research design for situation testing (Bendick, 1989). Cross et al. (1990) used a slightly adapted version of this design as part of a federal programme to study discrimination against job applicants of Hispanic origin. Shortly afterwards, the UI launched a parallel study on the experiences of black job applicants (Turner et al., 1991) and around the same time, the Fair Employment Council (FEC) initiated two parallel studies based on different adaptations of the original research design, which also covered black and Hispanic job applicants (Bendick et al., 1991; Bendick et al., 1993). Apart from differences in sample size and geographical coverage, these studies also differed in the details of the respective research design, thus making comparisons of their findings rather difficult.

The differences in research design in the various studies and the disparities in the findings have resulted in a certain amount of criticism, notably from specialists in social science research methodology. In an effort to develop the debate further and to promote the development of a reliable comparative research methodology, the Rockefeller Foundation brought researchers and critics together at a conference in Washington, DC in September 1991.[14]

The ILO project: the need for international, comparative research

When developing a situation testing methodology to match the demands of the ILO research project, certain factors relating to previous situation testing methodology had to be borne in mind. Hitherto, the methodology had only been used to test discrimination in certain countries and areas, in only a few, and not necessarily the most representative, sectors of the labour market and, furthermore, only against certain migrant or minority groups. Countries where a relatively great deal of research had been carried out tended to be those that shared Common Law traditions and this reflected these countries' high expectations of the law in solving social problems. Results of previous situation testing had sometimes been inconclusive or contradictory, since different types of research models and methodologies had been used. For example, testing had been carried out by correspondence, telephone and in person, sample sizes had varied, the tests had covered different stages of the application process, and so on. These factors made it difficult to compare the findings of the various studies and, as such, excluded the possibility for sound cross-country comparison.

To overcome such deficiencies and in an effort to take the next logical step in advancing research in discrimination, it was decided to: (a) initiate internationally comparative research in several countries; (b) base it on a standard research methodology; and (c) address common theoretical questions. This was among the prime objectives of the ILO's project, "Combating discrimination against (im)migrant workers and ethnic minorities in the world of work", which was implemented during the 1990s. The current methodology builds on previous experiences with situation testing and also builds on the debate between researchers and their critics at the Washington, DC conference.[15]

Designing a standard methodology that can be applied in different countries presents numerous challenges, since the differences between industrialized, migrant-receiving countries are huge: immigrant groups and economies differ and methods of recruiting personnel vary. A standard methodology needs to comprise a reasoned proposition as to the selection of equivalent entities in different countries in order to make comparisons meaningful. Obviously, this limits the amount of variables one can take into account in such an internationally applicable methodology.

Although it would have been preferable to base the research, like any research programme, on an elaborated and specified economic and social theory, this was not feasible, given the limited financial means and time span allocated for the research project. By closely analysing previous research, however, it was possible to list a series of relevant variables that might be connected with discrimination. Obviously, the longer the list, the more complex the research design would be. The introduction of each new independent variable would multiply the degree of difficulty of successfully carrying out the research and would also add to the cost. It was, therefore, decided that the list of potential variables to be included in the national research projects should be kept to the absolute minimum necessary to make a cross-cultural comparison of the research findings possible.

Potential research variables

The ILO's Discrimination (Employment and Occupation) Convention, 1958 (No. 111) defines discrimination as "... any distinction, exclusion or preference made on the basis of race, colour, sex, religion, political opinion, national extraction or social origin, which has the effect of nullifying or impairing equality of opportunity or treatment in employment or occupation".[16] Discrimination on the grounds of nationality is already laid down in the Migration for Employment Convention (Revised), 1949 (No. 97).[17] For the purposes of this research, discrimination is taken to mean specifically those practices that occur when migrants and ethnic minorities are accorded inferior treatment relative to representatives of the majority population in spite of comparable levels of education, qualifications and/or experience.

Discrimination in the world of work can take a wide range of forms: when hiring and firing staff and when considering employees for promotion.[18] It can consist of different levels of pay for the same work, assigning certain workers to the worst tasks within a job category, or it can reveal itself in disparities in other work conditions or financial fringe benefits. In order to keep the international research design manageable and the findings comparable, it was decided to measure the occurrence of discrimination in access to jobs only. In other words, the research only concerns itself with discrimination against immigrants and ethnic minorities in the hiring process.

The basic notions of discrimination presented above suggest that the following variables should be considered relevant. For each variable, two mutually exclusive propositions are given, reflecting the two extremes with regard to the expected effect of the respective variable.

Size of establishments

The first proposition is that small firms show fewer cases of discrimination because their simple hiring procedures make it easier for them to take the individual qualities of job applicants into account. As industrial relations might be paternalistic, minority employees might be more acceptable. The contrary proposition is that large firms have more room to experiment with exceptional individuals belonging to minority groups. They may generally feel obliged to show more responsibility to the community at large,[19] are more vulnerable to minority protest actions and are more closely watched by anti-discrimination law enforcement agencies.

Public and private sectors

Neoclassical economic reasoning predicts less discrimination in the private sector because employers who discriminate suffer from a comparative disadvantage when they restrict their choices when hiring personnel. Since, according to this theory, discrimination can only continue to occur in monopolistic situations of the economy and in the non-profit sector, it follows that discrimination should be higher in the public sector. The reverse proposition is that there is less discrimination in this sector, since government institutions abide strictly by anti-discrimination legislation. This implies that private-sector companies have more freedom in their hiring practices than public-sector firms.

Ethnic groups

According to the first proposition, discrimination should be highest against migrant groups that have already been residing in the country for a long time.

As members of the host society perceive these migrants as not having integrated well, they are thought of as "problem" groups. The alternate proposition is that employers reject those immigrants about whom they have the least information, in other words, newcomers. Whichever prediction proves to be true, it is probable that the degree of discrimination closely corresponds to the "social ranking" of the ethnic groups as shown by opinion polls.[20] Where social distance in society at large is governed by race, ethnic origin or national background, discrimination by employers is strongest against those who are thought of socially as constituting "distant" categories.

Gender

According to the first proposition, migrant and ethnic minority women face more discrimination than migrant and ethnic minority men. They are not just discriminated against because of their minority status but also because of their gender. Female migrants are thus a particularly disadvantaged group.[21] Migrant and ethic minority women may also face more discrimination than men because of their relatively lower educational levels, which are believed to make them suitable for only low-skilled work. The contrary proposition is that minority men are discriminated against more than minority women because their advancement in society is considered more of a threat to the predominantly male societal majority.

Jobs and educational level

The first proposition reasons that the higher the educational level, the less discrimination immigrants will encounter. As they do not fit the stereotype of the uneducated beginner and have shown that they can conform to the standards of their new society, they are treated as equals. Their ability to adapt is seen as a result of their education. The inverse proposition is that those who strive for social advancement through education are bound to lose out when they compete with majority applicants. As long as immigrants know their place and are made to carry out the kind of jobs that are rejected by the majority of native workers, they do not compete and, hence, do not threaten the fabric of society.[22]

Regional concentration of immigrants

It can be reasoned that as long as the number of immigrants in a given region is small, the less severe will be the discrimination against them. In these circumstances they are not seen as a threat to the established social system because they do not constitute a competitive force; on the contrary, tiny minority groups might even provide an element of exoticism. The opposite is true in the case of malignant racism and xenophobia. As a matter of principle, no immigrants are to be accepted. Employing them is seen as constituting a first step towards mass settlement and *Überfremdung* ("over-foreignization").

Economic variation

Under economic conditions where demand for labour is high and supply is low, discrimination can be expected to be far less than in areas where demand is low and the labour supply high. Thus in regions with a tight labour market, in expanding economic sectors, or in certain professions where demand is high, little discrimination should be expected. However, if discrimination is of the malignant type, economic demand and supply ratios cannot be expected to make any difference to its occurrence.

Selecting research variables

An ideal research design should include at least all of the seven variables presented above, and there are others still that might also influence the outcome of a discrimination test. Test results are only truly comprehensive when all possible variables are taken into account. But carrying out such a research project would be virtually impossible as it would require impracticably large samples to meet the basic requirements of statistical relevance. Accordingly, in the research design drawn up for the ILO's international project many of the variables were dropped in order to limit the methodological and financial problems inherent in carrying out comparable research in different countries. The following selection of criteria represents a basis for providing a methodologically sound answer to the question as to whether discrimination against immigrants and ethnic minorities is such a widespread phenomenon that it can be assumed to contribute to the creation of societies in which inequality is also based on ethnic differences.

- In each country, the research project should include a test of discrimination against at least two large migrant and ethnic minority groups.
- The research should cover access to jobs at the semi-skilled level for low-skilled first-generation immigrants and should cover access to jobs at the skilled level for relatively well-educated, second-generation migrants or members of a well-established ethnic minority.

- The test should cover minority males only. Although it would make sense to include tests for discrimination against both men and women, this would more than double the research design, since all the other variables might be expected to vary. In order to keep the research manageable and financially feasible, a choice had to be made between the two sexes. Because male migrant workers are more numerous than female migrant workers in the countries to be covered, it was decided to limit the tests to male job applicants.
- The research should focus on job applicants in the 20–25 age group, since migrants and ethnic minorities make up relatively young segments of the overall population.
- The occurrence of discrimination should be measured for entry-level jobs.
- The tests should be administered in regions with relatively high concentrations of migrant and ethnic minority workers and where demand for labour was relatively high.
- The tests should focus on access to semi-skilled jobs in industry and in services because it was felt that, in these economic sectors, where minority and majority workers compete for jobs, discrimination was most likely to occur. These are also the situations in which immigrants and ethnic minorities are most likely to find themselves. In the countries covered by the research, unskilled jobs in these sectors, as well as in agriculture, tend to be dominated by migrants and ethnic minorities; in other words, there is little or no competition with native, majority group workers and, therefore, no possibility of testing whether discrimination occurs at the point of hiring.
- In countries where a sizeable number of second-generation migrants and ethnic minorities already existed and where these migrants had been through the national school system and a sizeable number of them had attained higher vocational or college diplomas, the test should focus on access to skilled jobs.
- As the decision on whether to focus on private- and/or public-sector jobs largely depends on the requirements for access to the public service (in some countries non-nationals are not eligible), no overall recommendation could be made.
- With respect to the size of establishments, it was expected that relevant data on company size might not be easy to collect within the framework of the situation tests. However, as most job opportunities occur in small and medium-sized firms, it was expected that these firms would be over-represented in the final sample of job vacancies tested.

Of the countries covered in this study, discrimination in access to both semi-skilled and skilled jobs could only be tested in Germany and the

Netherlands. Due to financial constraints, the research in Belgium and Spain covered only access to semi-skilled jobs. The standard methodology for applications for skilled jobs could only be followed accurately in the Netherlands.[23] This study, therefore, only covers the standardized methodology used for testing discrimination in access to semi-skilled jobs[24] and reports on the test results in all of the four countries covered: Belgium, Germany, the Netherlands and Spain. The variables that were retained for the international research project examined in this study can thus be summarized as follows:

- The research would test discrimination at the entry level for semi-skilled jobs.
- The research would measure the occurrence of discrimination against second-generation migrant and minority males in the 20–25 age group.
- The research would be carried out in regions where relatively high concentrations of the selected migrant and minority groups had settled and in areas with a relatively strong demand for labour and within the industry and services sectors of the economy.

General description of the technique

Situation testing for discrimination in access to employment is a social experiment in real-life situations where people in positions of power make decisions about people who apply to them for jobs. Both members of the team of testers followed exactly the same procedure when they applied for the same semi-skilled job. They could make an unsolicited approach to a prospective employer in person, or apply by telephone. They could apply for work at employment agencies, both private and public, and they could look for permanent or temporary employment. The general principle was that they should follow the usual procedures for the type of jobs and applications being tested. Since the testers were to present themselves in person, it was essential that the individuals making up each team were similarly matched as to characteristics and qualifications.

Should the testers work in pairs or threes? Researchers in some countries have been able to test relative discrimination against more than one minority group, so it was tempting to use a team of three testers rather than just two. In Australia, for example, levels of discrimination against Vietnamese as well as Greeks have been tested by matching Vietnamese, Greek and Anglo-Saxon testers, who then operated in threes.[25] However, there is a danger that employers faced with three applicants of strikingly similar qualifications in a short time span would become suspicious. The possibility for detection, which is always present in situation tests, had to be kept to a minimum. Any public disclosure that followed detection would ruin the entire experiment. So it was decided that only pairs of testers would be used.

It was of crucial importance that the two testers making up each team were virtually interchangeable – in age, education, work experience and so on. They needed to be dressed similarly and be equally "presentable". The only difference allowed between the two was that one had to come from an immigrant or ethnic minority background and the other – the control tester – from the majority population. It was essential that the personnel managers or other decision-makers of the randomly selected firms came face to face with two equally qualified applicants and that they should respond to them in exactly the same way, that is, by hiring or rejecting both or by preferring one to the other. If the latter occurred on a significantly large scale to rule out chance, the differential treatment could only be attributed to discrimination, because the only appreciable difference between the carefully matched candidates would be race or ethnic background.

It should be stressed that this type of research does not focus on (or at best only indirectly) on immigrants and ethnic minorities. Rather, it studies whether or not employers or their representatives engage in discrimination. As such, and given the fact that these decision-makers are, by definition, virtually all representatives of the majority population, this study looks at the behaviour of the majority population. Essential to this type of research is that the people who are being studied are unaware that they are being observed, for only then can the test results be considered representative of everyday life. However, this type of research does not study individual cases; it gathers together the aggregate data of sufficiently large samples so that the influence of chance can be ruled out. If the number of times that the minority applicant is rejected and the majority applicant is accepted is statistically often enough to rule out chance, then the proof offered for the occurrence of discrimination can be considered statistically valid.

Because it was technically unfeasible to pursue all the tests into the final stage, it is reasonable to assume that the level of discrimination that actually takes place is higher than that yielded by the research methodology. Moreover, it should be remembered that the situation testing technique is limited to investigating discrimination in access to employment only. Instances of discriminatory treatment in employment or in decisions with respect to firing cannot be appraised by this method. As a consequence, the actual amount of discrimination in employment is bound to be higher than that revealed by the situation testing.

Selection and preparation of the testers

The selection procedure

In all four countries, the tests were to be carried out by at least two teams of two males between the ages of 20 and 25. One individual from each team had to belong to the ethnic background being used to test discrimination at the semi-skilled work level, the other had to belong to the majority population. Each was required to look like an average jobseeker of conventional appearance. It was decided to use university students rather than professional actors, as in some previous research studies, since the experience with students had been quite satisfactory and they are also less expensive. Furthermore, instructing them about the theoretical background and the technical administration of the tests would be easier. An advertisement requesting young men between the ages of 20 and 25 willing to participate in an experiment on job applications, particularly students of ethnic minority background, was circulated.

Subsequently, the researchers selected ten students of a conventional appearance and who, at first sight, looked like the sort of person who would be seeking semi-skilled work. From these ten, four were engaged as testers by a researcher and an expert consultant from the nearest national employment agency office. Two of the testers needed to originate from the minority group to be tested and two from the majority group. All four needed to be inter-changeable, so that reliability checks could be carried out to exclude tester bias. First and family names were chosen to match names typical of the ethnic background of the testers. All four applicants were required to have the same legal status: the foreign immigrants were to present themselves as having all the necessary permits to qualify them for an appointment on an equal basis to nationals.

The four selected testers needed to be interchangeable in such objective characteristics as age, weight, height and command of the language, and, if necessary, had to possess a driving licence. They were also required to be similar in subjective characteristics, such as communicative ability, general behaviour and appearance. It was recommended that the selected testers be more or less average in these respects; they should not be exceptionally pleasing, open and endearing nor offensive, annoying or unusually self-contained. The rationale was that the most pleasing of both majority and minority applicants as well as the most disagreeable would provoke the same sort of response from the employer. If one was dealing with non-malignant discrimination, both the pleasant testers would be accepted and both the unpleasant ones would be rejected. In that case, the study would be measuring individual variability of acceptance rather than the discrimination of categories of people.

A danger in all scientific experiments is the occurrence of so-called "experimenter effects". In the case of this particular research, this might take the form of individuals keen to prove to the world that horrendous discrimination does exist by inducing, through their behaviour (consciously or unconsciously), more negative responses from employers than individuals who had set out to prove (again, consciously or not) that the problem of discrimination was being exaggerated. As the direct observers in these tests were themselves also the experimental stimuli, a way of avoiding this problem would have been to keep the testers ignorant of the subject of the research. They would then have neither induced the outcome of the tests nor influenced each other. However, this would have been impracticable; the researchers would not have been able to train the testers together or teach them how to behave and respond in exactly the same manner.

In an attempt to rule out tester bias, it was recommended that the testers should not be selected from circles with outspoken views on discrimination: they should not be recruited from either anti-discrimination organizations or from racist political parties. Furthermore, their individual life histories should be checked; it would be unwise to select individuals who had themselves been victims of serious discrimination or people with a criminal record. To avoid further tester bias, the testers were to be hired for the full duration of the testing period, and paid a regular salary – not paid according to the number of tests they completed or by an hourly rate. This would avoid them stopping before the end of the test period or extending the process unnecessarily. In other words, it was essential that the testers be paid for their participation in the research, irrespective of the outcome of the tests in which they participated.

Training

It was considered necessary to train the testers for a minimum period of one week and according to a standard curriculum before they went "into the field". On day one, the research design was to be explained. On day two each tester was taught how to modify his personal history to fit the profile designed for each type of vacancy to be tested. It was recommended that they stick as closely as possible to the truth as fewer mistakes would then be made. The testers were instructed to keep their dates of birth, addresses and other basic information about themselves constant. Only their biographies were modified to reflect the relevant education and training experience required for the jobs, in other words, their citizenship, birthplace, work experience and hobbies. Job references needed to be prepared. When the respective biographies were constructed, it was recommended that the testers choose the highest possible qualifications that fitted the job concerned in order to maximize the likelihood of both testers being considered equally suitable for the job.

The third and fourth days of instruction were set aside to training the testers' individual behaviour, in particular teaching them how to act courteously and how to respond to the employers' questions. The students were expected to appreciate this part of the training the most, as they were, in essence, being given a free course in job applications. Most of the national employment agencies in the countries included in this research project offer professional training programmes, and these were used for this part of the training process. It was also suggested that an experienced personnel manager be brought in to help. This part of the training was expected to last two days as it involved the students not only learning how to present themselves at their best, but also how to give off a consistent image of themselves. This was important as the credibility of the tests depended on the degree to which all the controllable test variables were kept constant. The final day was assigned to ensuring that all the testers understood how to follow the scheduling and data collection procedures.

Handling psychological problems

The researchers were alerted to the fact that some of the testers might be distressed at their first encounters with discrimination and also later on in the research procedure, should the systematic nature of discrimination become apparent. As mentioned in the previous chapter, potential victims of discrimination tend to be unaware of or underestimate the degree of discrimination that actually takes place. When an employer rejects a tester tactlessly by not concealing the fact that the individual is considered to be of the "wrong" race, this may be the first time the tester has met such discrimination. And it can be even worse when the tester finds out that an attentive and pleasant employer who rejects the tester's application because the vacancy has "regrettably just been filled" gives the job to the majority tester just 15 minutes later. "I can hardly understand it! He was such a nice man. I never would have expected him to be racist" commented some testers in previous research undertaken by Bovenkerk. Discussing these problems was not only important on compassionate grounds; if not properly counselled, the testers might lose their open-mindedness and actually induce discrimination by their appearance and/or behaviour in the remaining tests, resulting in unacceptable tester bias. It was, therefore, necessary to monitor the testers continuously during the course of the research to check their feelings and motivation. It was always a possibility that a tester who could no longer handle the discrimination might need to be replaced.

The tests

The statistical basis for sampling consisted of all the vacancies available for semi-skilled jobs in the industrial and services sectors within the geographical area chosen for the investigation. The researchers were instructed that the occupations chosen should represent the type of jobs in which the majority of young adults would begin their working careers. A uniform set of instructions about exactly what kind of semi-skilled job vacancies to select for testing was impossible to give as these vary between countries and even within individual countries over a relatively short span of time. It was, therefore, suggested that the researchers check all the data available on the supply of and demand for labour in the given region and then decide whether to concentrate on the construction sector or on light industry, on the hotel and restaurant business or on whatever sector of the labour market would present suitable vacancies during the research period. It was also suggested that the researchers consult with the regional offices of each country's national employment agency. It was stressed that the largest possible variation over the industrial and services sectors should be achieved so as to avoid testing one limited sector only. However, the degree of representation both within the sectors and for the sectors at large would be limited by the availability of vacancies for testing. The researchers were advised to try to reduce the testable situations to a limited set of semi-skilled jobs for which detailed professional profiles could be obtained. This would make it easier to construct adequate profiles for the testers, which, in turn, would enhance their chances of being considered for the vacancies concerned. The following distribution of vacancies was suggested:

- 50 observations in the construction industry, at the levels of bricklayers and carpenters
- 50 observations in the restaurant business as an experienced waiter
- 50 observations in light production industries as a semi-skilled worker
- 25 observations in the retail sector

Finding vacancies

How do people looking for jobs go about finding suitable vacancies? There are three basic avenues:

- Through personal contacts: relatives, friends, acquaintances or the ethnic or regional network
- By direct application at the factory gate or responding to signs and notices in employers' windows stating "help wanted"

- Through intermediaries:

  - Advertisements in newspapers
  - National employment agencies
  - Commercial temporary employment services

Within the framework of situation tests it is technically impossible to find suitable vacancies through personal contacts. The required network of knowledge and recommendations cannot be manipulated experimentally to match the two testers. The other options, however, remained open. The testers could apply directly to an employer, for instance, at the factory gate or at a shop, whenever this was local custom. Job offers published in the local and regional press provided another possibility. A theoretical way of using the national employment agency was to register as a jobseeker and to wait and see what was offered.

It was decided not to pursue the latter strategy because it would have produced no more than one or a few vacancies at a time and the same vacancies might not necessarily be offered to the two testers. Seeking the national employment agency's collaboration in selecting vacancies for the two testers might have been possible in some countries, but could equally well have been impossible in others. National employment agencies usually depend on the willingness of employers to report vacancies to them, and they might not want to jeopardize their relations with the employers who use their services.

Finally, there was the option of using commercial temporary employment services. Experience has shown that practice tests are easy to administer through this channel.[27] The main argument against using these services is that they only mediate between employers and applicants for temporary work. However, many workers start on a temporary basis and end up being employed permanently. More employers are now using these types of agencies, particularly during slack labour-market conditions when they prefer to hire personnel on a probationary basis. Since conditions are flexible, temporary employment agencies provide a good point of entry for people to semi-skilled jobs. At the time that the research project took place, Spain was the only country in which commercial temporary services were not permitted to operate. However, since the integrity of the international research is best safeguarded when the testers use the same sort of channels that real jobseekers would usually follow in their own country, it was decided to include temporary employment services as a means of finding suitable vacancies, whenever this corresponded to national or local practice.

Statistical analysis and sample size

The situation tests were based on the inductive statistics model of the binomial distribution used for testing two conflicting hypotheses.[28] The hypothesis that is actually tested is often referred to as the null hypothesis (H_0) in contrast to the research hypothesis (H_1). These two mutually exclusive hypotheses can be elaborated as follows:

- H_0: Job application procedures will not be biased against one or the other job applicant. They will be treated equally.
- H_1: Job application procedures will be biased against one or the other job applicants. They will be treated unequally, that is, one will be discriminated against.

Because many of the findings of previous situation testing have been contested on the grounds of the small sample used, the sample size used in this research was considered to be of prime importance. Accordingly, the size of the sample to be used would be required to be reasoned on the basis of statistical assumptions. The research method used was based on two assumptions. Firstly, that both applicants would be rejected in 50 per cent of all the vacancies tested. The total sample of all the tested vacancies would constitute the group of all valid applications. In the remaining 50 per cent, either both or only one of the applicants would be accepted. This group constituted the collection of usable observations (N) for the situation test. It is upon this sample of usable observations that the test's computations were based.

Secondly, it was decided that it would be necessary to obtain a minimum difference of inequality in treatment between the two groups tested of 15 per cent in order to conclude that the difference in treatment found was not due to pure chance. This 15 per cent of differential treatment was the minimum proportion or critical rate (CR), below which it was accepted that the occurrence of discrimination could not be verified statistically. At a significance level of 5 per cent, any overall net discrimination rate that was higher than or equal to 15 per cent would result in a rejection of the null hypothesis of equal treatment of both testers. This required minimum net discrimination rate would, for instance, be arrived at if the majority tester had been favoured in 25 per cent of the cases of unequal treatment and the minority tester in 10 per cent of these cases $(25\%-10\% = 15\%)$.

The next question that needed to be addressed was how large the sample size of usable tests should be if a net discrimination rate of 15 per cent is to be due to pure chance in less than 5 per cent out of a hundred tests. If (P) represents the proportion of net discrimination in real life and (p) the proportion of net discrimination in the research sample, then the difference between the two should be smaller than 0.15∂ (∂ being the standard unit of the normal distribution) in 0.95 ($1.0–0.05$) per cent of the tests. If the total number of usable cases, N, is sufficiently large, the Bernouilli-distribution can be assumed to equal the normal distribution. 0.95 then equals a value of 1.96:

$$Prob\ ([P–p] < .15\partial) = 0.95$$
$$0.15\partial = 1.96\ \partial p$$

On the assumption that the standard normal distribution $\partial p = \partial / \sqrt{N}$ would be applicable, the equation becomes:

$$0.15\partial = 1.96\partial / \sqrt{N}$$
$$\sqrt{N} = 1.96\partial / 0.15\partial$$
$$\sqrt{N} = 170$$

To summarize: in order to meet the requirements of statistical validity, the sample of usable cases, N, should be at least 170, in which case the required minimum net discrimination rate would be 15 per cent. It was recommended that the minimum number of N be set at 175. A test result that reached or surpassed a net discrimination rate of 15 per cent in that case would provide incontrovertible proof that discrimination had occurred. The total sample size of vacancies tested, that is, the valid cases that included the application procedures in which both testers got immediately rejected before even the first phase of the procedure (see below), should be estimated at double the amount of the required valid cases, or 350. When the total number of usable tests reached 175, the actual test procedure could be discontinued. On the basis of the formula used for calculating the total number of usable tests required for the overall sample in any given country, it was possible to calculate the required minimum net discrimination rate in specific sub-samples, for example, within specific regions, sectors and/or occupations, where the number of usable tests to be taken into account is lower than 175. As N decreases, the required CR will go up on the assumption that the significance level is kept at 5 per cent:

$$CR = 1.96 / \sqrt{N}$$

The application process

Employers who discriminate may do so in the early stages of the hiring process, but they may also discriminate as the process approaches the actual hiring decision. A full measure of discrimination in access to employment therefore demands that eventual unequal treatment should be measured during all the stages of the application process. The final score of discrimination is the cumulative result of rejections of one tester where the other is accepted. For the purposes of the testing procedure, the tests were discontinued as soon as one or both testers had been rejected.

There are three basic steps in every application procedure (see figure 1.1):

- Jobseekers apply for a vacancy by showing up in person or by telephoning ("Is this job still available?"). Their application may be taken into consideration or they may be denied a chance to apply ("We're sorry, the job has just been taken.").
- Applicants may then be given the chance to present their credentials, after which they may or may not be invited for an interview ("Sorry, we're looking for somebody with different qualifications.").
- The interview may result in an actual job offer or a rejection.

In other words, the procedure specified three stages at which one of the two team members could be rejected or accepted because of the prospective employer making a choice between the two. At this point, the procedure came to an end. A measure of discrimination or inequality of treatment would have been obtained in one of the three stages.

Figure 1.1   Stages in the application procedure

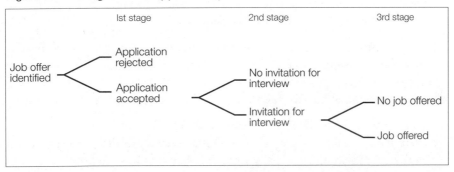

Once the job vacancy was identified, the first stage of the procedure began. The two testers making up a team each telephoned to apply for the job and indicated their willingness to attend an interview to demonstrate their suitability for the job in question. The prescribed interval between telephone calls was about ten minutes and for each new application the order in which the testers applied was changed so as to avoid any possibility that a preference for the first caller would benefit one of the two applicants. It was essential that during the telephone call it should be made clear through the applicant's name that the person in question was either a representative of the majority population or a representative of the migrant or minority group selected.

There were then several possible outcomes:

(a) Both applications were rejected (the job had just been given to someone else; neither of the two applicants were thought suitable).
(b) Both applications were accepted (both were suitable, but in some cases they might be placed on a waiting list, together with a number of other applicants and would "be contacted"; in other cases, both of the candidates were invited to present their credentials, in which case they moved on to the second stage).
(c) Only one of the applications was accepted, either that of the national or that of the migrant/minority applicant.

In situations (a) and (c), the procedure came to an end for both testers. Situation (a) represented cases that were valid but inadequate for the measurement of discrimination. In situation (c), only one applicant was rejected and the other one was accepted. As this constituted clear difference of treatment, these tests could be discontinued. Cases that fell under situation (b) moved on to the second stage, and could lead to one of the following:

(a) Neither of the two was invited for an interview.
(b) Both were invited for an interview and they went on to the third stage.
(c) Only one of them was invited for an interview.
(d) They were both requested to send in a curriculum vitae, and a reply was promised but nothing actually happened.

In situations (a), (c) and (d), the procedure ended for both of the testers; situation (c) represented a clear example of unequal treatment. The third stage applied only to cases that fell under situation (b) of the second stage. The result here could mean that the two testers were requested to come for an interview:

(a) Neither went for an interview (because it was stipulated that they demonstrate their mastery of the required skills or because the job was located more than 100 kilometres away from the operations base, etc).
(b) Both went for an interview but neither was offered a job.
(c) Both went for an interview and both were offered a job.
(d) Both went for an interview but only one was offered a job.

In all these cases the testing procedure came to end. Only situation (d) could be counted as a case of unequal treatment.

It should be pointed out, though, that rather more subtle types of discrimination could be meted out to the two testers than a clear-cut case of acceptance or rejection demonstrates. For instance, both could be offered a job but not on the same conditions. In research carried out by the Urban Institute, for example, a case is referred to in which a black tester and a white tester applied for a job as a car salesman: the white tester was offered a job in new car sales, whereas the black tester was told that the only available job was in used car sales (Turner et al., 1991).

Which test results represent discrimination?

How can differences in treatment be interpreted? Disparate treatment can result from systematic behaviour, such as discrimination, or from random events, such as an employer's bad mood. It is possible that disparate treatment is entirely related to systematic behaviour, random events, or to a combination of the two. In order to measure discrimination, the cases of unfavourable treatment of the majority tester should be subtracted from those in which the minority tester was treated unfavourably, so as to arrive at a value of "net disparate treatment". The assumption underlying this method is that random events are cancelled out by the subtraction and that the difference accounts for systematic behaviour. The approach assumes that random unfavourable treatment is symmetrical for majority and minority test outcomes.

Differences in treatment were often straightforward – one tester was rejected and the other was accepted at one of the three stages of the application process. But differences in treatment also took other forms. Some were measurable, others too subtle to quantify. A difference in the timing of an invitation to an interview could be measured: one applicant was ranked lower in the selection process. Another difference in treatment that emerged was that one person was offered the job but the other's name was kept on file should a future vacancy turn up. Still another was that both got a job but the conditions offered to each were different. These experiences were gleaned from the diaries kept for each test. Clearly, the evidence of discrimination in these instances, although measurable, was less "concrete" than a straightforward difference between rejection and acceptance. The former resulted in the absolute minimum outcome of the tests, that is, the minimum rate of discrimination that was proven beyond any doubt, whereas the latter constituted the maximum rate of observed net discrimination.

Supervision

The implementation of the practice tests required the continuous presence of a fieldwork supervisor. The supervisor scheduled all the work, monitored the testers' progress, recorded all the findings and kept them on file. In order to avoid the experimenter effects mentioned earlier in this chapter, the supervisor had to carry out validity checks at regular intervals to ensure that the test findings were not biased.[29]

The supervisor was instructed to select vacancies according to the sample stratification and to draw up a list of firms to be tested. The tests were to be scheduled on a day-by-day basis, enabling the supervisor to prepare the testers for each application separately. Each day's proceedings started with telephone inquiries being made about the availability of the jobs selected. The conversations took place in the supervisor's presence and were taped. All instances of testing required close timing, as it was necessary that the employer consider the two testers' applications together; ten-minute intervals between the calls was considered best. The order in which the two testers executed their tasks was changed every time in order to ensure that a disparate outcome was not due to one of the testers always having been first.

When the testers were asked to present themselves in person, the supervisor followed them to ensure that the testers did in fact carry out their tests and did not make up the results. This may seem a superfluous and slightly ludicrous procedure, but anyone familiar with survey research using interviewees will know that it is a necessary precaution.

In cases where the test did not begin with a telephone call, the supervisor went along in a car and provided a temporary research base near the site of the test. The supervisor closely monitored the movements and behaviour of the testers and checked the motivation of the testers from time to time, so that any psychological problems were spotted well in advance. After each point of contact, the testers wrote down in detail what had happened on a standardized report form. They checked with the supervisor at the end of their day's testing and handed in their filled-in forms. The supervisor kept a file of the proceedings of the two testers for each vacancy. The testing for a specific vacancy was discontinued by the supervisor as soon as one of the testers was rejected. The overall testing procedure was stopped when a total of 175 usable team observations had been collected.

A note on ethical considerations

The use of situation tests for both research and law enforcement purposes has been criticized on ethical grounds. It has often been claimed, for example, that the research method departs from the normal prerequisite in the social sciences that research be based on the informed consent of the subjects studied and that this method thus infringes on a person's privacy.[30] This criticism can be countered, however, by pointing out that hiring is, ultimately, a public act. In most instances, the job vacancies tested were advertised publicly and the behaviour of the employers or other decision-makers was, therefore, regulated, either by legislation barring discrimination or by professional codes of conduct.

The hiring of personnel can, therefore, not be regarded as an entirely private matter. Employers and their representatives are not free to exclude job applicants on inappropriate grounds, that is, grounds that are not relevant to the job, such as race or ethnic origin.

Moreover, situation testing involves no real harm or liability for the firm or employee being tested. The situation testing research methodology for the ILO project was constructed in such a way as to make it as unobtrusive as possible and to occupy as little time as possible. The research does not report on the individual behaviour of employers, nor were they enticed to engage in illegal behaviour. In fact, the purpose of the tests is to observe the conventional practices of the firm or organization tested and not to stimulate exceptional behaviour. Any concern that researchers might be breaking entrapment laws is misconceived: employers who discriminate are breaking the law, not the researchers. But, more importantly: the testers are only observing conventional practices; they are not luring employers into a situation in which they are encouraged to deviate from their normal course of action. It should also be pointed out that the pool of legitimate applicants was not affected, since the tests were discontinued as soon as one tester had been discriminated against or as soon as a job offer had been made.

Fix and Struyk (1993) state that the legitimacy of situation testing is reinforced by the simple fact that there is no analytical alternative for determining the prevalence of discrimination, just as there is no alternative to the clandestine character of the research. To request the consent of individual employers would lead to staged behaviour and would thus defeat the object of the methodology. In short, the problem of ethics, if it is to be raised at all, applies more to the perpetrators of unlawful discrimination than to researchers bringing this behaviour to the attention of policy-makers and the public.[31] Indeed, it is precisely this type of research that has exerted a strong influence on the development and subsequent refinement of public policies aimed at counteracting illegal, unethical discrimination.

Notes

[1] Based on Bovenkerk (1992), with additional research by Zegers de Beijl.

[2] The ILO (1998) argues that the concept of "race" has long been exposed as a fallacy and as scientifically void. The term "race" continues to be widely used, including in international and national law, and its derivative "racial discrimination" has come to mean discrimination on the grounds of perceived race, as opposed to actual race, which does not exist. Acknowledging that "race" is a subjective concept, throughout this study the term "race" should be read as "perceived race" and "racial discrimination" as "discrimination based on the grounds of perceived race". For the sake of presentation, quotation marks are not used with the terms. The ILO's Committee of Experts on the Application of Conventions and Recommendations have adopted a similar position (see the ILO, 1996), and this study follows its example. For a discussion of the genesis, scientific debates and subsequent downgrading of the concept, see Banton and Harwood (1975).

Documenting discrimination against migrant workers

[3] See, for example, Jenkins (1986) and Kirschenman and Neckerman (1991).

[4] See Bovenkerk and Breuning-van Leeuwen (1978) and Newman and Krzystofiak (1979).

[5] A striking example can be found in Essed (1991).

[6] In some countries, notably Canada, the Netherlands, the United Kingdom and the United States, legislation allows for discrimination or unequal treatment within the framework of affirmative action programmes, which aim to remove existing discriminatory barriers and disadvantages so as to achieve factual equality of opportunity for groups that are under-represented in employment. For more details, see the ILO (1998).

[7] The results of the PEP report, showing substantial levels of discrimination against the West Indian and Hungarian applicants, can be found in Daniel (1968).

[8] Fourteen years later the same test was applied in the same city, Nottingham. See Simpson and Stevenson (1994).

[9] The same conclusion was drawn by Büyükbozkoyum et al. (1991) as a result of a small-sample correspondence test against highly educated engineers of Turkish descent.

[10] Bovenkerk et al. (1979) used situation testing to provide evidence of discrimination in access to employment against males of Antillean descent in France.

[11] The results of a later test carried out by Henry (1989) challenged the earlier findings. The drop in discrimination that was evident in the second study may have been due to substantial labour shortages and because of the small sample used. Henry also reported substantial levels of negative treatment of coloured, foreign-born testers – lack of courtesy, the querying of job credentials, and so forth. Her interpretation of the research findings generated lively debate. See Raskin (1993) and Ventura (1995).

[12] Like other researchers before them, Riach and Rich hypothesized that the extent of discrimination is influenced by unemployment levels, in other words, demand for and supply of labour in different sectors of the labour market.

[13] On the methodological inadequacies of Newman's research and for a discussion of three other small-scale studies carried out before 1990 in the United States, see Bendick (1996). For a detailed overview of all situation tests carried out in the United States up to the early 1990s, covering, inter alia, access to employment, housing, credits and so on, see Fix and Struyk (1993).

[14] The Conference papers were published in Fix and Struyk (1993).

[15] ibid.

[16] Discrimination (Employment and Occupation) Convention, 1958 (No. 111), art. 1(a).

[17] Migration for Employment Convention (Revised), 1949 (No. 97), art. 6.1.

[18] For an overview of discriminatory practices in the whole of the employment process in European countries, see Zegers de Beijl (1990).

[19] On the concept of corporate responsibility in relation to immigrant and ethnic minority workers, see Lindburg (1998), p. 5.

[20] For a recent example, see the European Commission (1998), which reports the results of a EU-wide survey that uncovered a worrying level of racism and xenophobia with nearly one-third of all respondents identifying themselves as "quite racist" or "very racist". Many of those interviewed agreed that the rights of those immigrants considered "problem groups" should be limited. Almost half the respondents thought that their respective country would be better off without migrants from outside the EU and one in five declared themselves to be in favour of repatriating all non-EU immigrants to their countries of origin.

[21] In this respect, Lim (1996), p. 99, emphasizes four points that increase the vulnerability of female migrants. They are vulnerable by virtue of: (a) being women vis-à-vis men; (b) being a migrant vis-à-vis non-migrant men and women; (c) being a foreigner vis-à-vis nationals; and (d) being undocumented (as is relatively often the case) vis-à-vis documented migrants.

[22] For a detailed discussion of this concept, see Böhning (1995).

[23] See Goldberg and Mourinho (1996) for an explanation of the methodological problems encountered in Germany when carrying out written applications for skilled jobs.

[24] See Bovenkerk (1992) for the complete research methodology, including instructions for correspondence testing for skilled jobs.

[25] See Riach and Rich (1992).

[26] See Bovenkerk (1992), p. 21.

[27] See Meloen (1991).

[28] See Blalock (1972).

[29] See Bovenkerk (1992), pp. 30–31, for detailed instructions on the carrying out of validity checks by means of a chi square test.

[30] See Reynolds (1979) on this norm in the social sciences.

[31] See Banton (1997) for an illuminating critique of the reasons put forward by the Swedish Social Research Council advising their Government not to participate in the ILO research project.

THE OCCURRENCE OF DISCRIMINATION IN BELGIUM

2

Bernadette Smeesters, Peter Arrijn, Serge Feld and André Nayer[1]

Immigration and the socio-economic position of migrant and ethnic minority groups

The organized migration of labour to Belgium took off immediately after the Second World War, when additional workers were needed to fill acute labour shortages in the coal-mining and iron and steel industries. The Belgian Government first concluded an agreement to recruit foreign workers with Italy, and this was later followed by agreements with Spain and then Greece. The rapid economic growth of the 1960s gave rise to additional agreements with Morocco and Turkey. Subsequently, in an effort to remedy the continuing shortages of manpower, especially of unskilled labour, immigration regulations were relaxed: many migrants entered the country on an irregular basis or overstayed tourist visas but were granted work and residence permits once they had found employment (Zegers de Beijl, 1990).

As in many other western European countries, the recruitment of unskilled migrant workers ceased in 1974. Since then, the increase in the foreign population in Belgium has been mainly due to the birth rate of resident foreigners, to families being reunited and to the formation of new families. The recruitment of new migrant workers has, by contrast, been confined to highly skilled workers from other industrialized countries, such as Japan and the United States. In 1996, the total foreign population of Belgium stood at 911,900, or 9 per cent of the total population. Of these, more than 60 per cent are nationals of other EU Member States, with Italians making up by far the largest group. As for foreigners from outside the EU, Moroccan nationals are the largest single group: they make up 15 per cent of all foreigners, followed by Turks (9 per cent). Naturalization has been increasing annually since 1992, when Belgium liberalized its naturalization requirements. In 1996, almost 25,000 foreigners were naturalized, of whom roughly one-third were of

Moroccan origin (Organisation for Economic Co-operation and Development [OECD], 1998).

According to the most recent census data (1991), the overall proportion of foreign workers in the economically active population is 8.3 per cent. Most migrant workers have been channelled into semi-skilled or unskilled jobs in the industrial, construction and service sectors. Wrench (1996) reports that Maghrebi and Turkish workers, in particular, tend to be employed below their real skills level and follow fragmented and insecure career paths. According to the census data, the proportion of unemployed people among national workers numbers 10.1 per cent, but among non-national workers the figure more than doubles (23.2 per cent). A general rise in unemployment levels since the beginning of the 1990s has affected all nationalities, but particularly foreign workers from non-EU countries. Moroccan and Turkish workers, especially, are both proportionately and in absolute terms severely affected by long-term unemployment. As Wrench notes:

The uneven distribution of foreigners and immigrants, by comparison with Belgian workers, becomes apparent when sectors and enterprises are undergoing restructuring, and in the case of mass redundancies and enterprise closures. Immigrants are often disproportionately concentrated in ... old heavy industries, vulnerable to closure.[2]

To what extent can the disproportionately high unemployment rate of migrant workers be attributed to the closure or restructuring of labour-intensive heavy industries in which they have traditionally been employed? The findings of the situation tests on the occurrence of discrimination in Belgium in access to employment should help answer this question.

Description of the testing procedure

Young workers of Moroccan descent were the reference group chosen for the situation tests in Belgium. As stated above, Moroccans form the largest single group of foreigners from non-EU countries. As they account for by far the highest rates of naturalization, it was decided not to present the testers as foreigners but as nationals. It was assumed that any eventual discrimination on the formal grounds of foreign nationality could thus be excluded from the test results. In other words, by choosing young nationals of foreign descent, the rate of discrimination to be uncovered would probably be lower than that experienced by workers who are, legally speaking, foreigners. Before the tests were carried out, circumstantial evidence already existed that workers of Moroccan nationality or origin, in particular, were being discriminated against in the world of work, although the extent of these problems was open to widely divergent claims.[3]

Belgium is a highly decentralized federal state, with large institutional, economic, demographic and linguistic differences in which, inter alia, policies with respect to employment fall largely under the authority of the three constituent regions – Brussels, Flanders and Wallonia. Therefore, it was decided to carry out the situation tests in each of the three regions separately, with the three teams of researchers nevertheless working closely together and harmonizing their procedures.

The tests were conducted in the Brussels area and in the agglomerations of Antwerp and Liège for the Flemish and Walloon regions respectively. They took place over two successive periods: from February to June 1996 and from October 1996 to February 1997. During and between these two periods, validity checks were carried out to exclude any tester bias. The researchers defined common criteria for valid and usable test findings, for distinguishing between direct and more subtle forms of discrimination by employers, and developed common procedures for data processing, taking into account regional differences with respect to job application and recruitment methods. For example, as the labour market in semi-skilled jobs is extremely slack in Flanders and Wallonia, it is not uncommon for jobseekers to make unsolicited applications – a jobseeking method that was incorporated in the total number of usable tests in these regions. On the other hand, as job vacancies are far more numerous in the Brussels area, testers could rely on job advertisements alone.

The testers were recruited from the population of university students in Antwerp, Brussels and Liège, through employment agencies and advertisements. Following a rigorous selection procedure, in which particular attention was paid to the composition of the pairs of testers and their similarity from the point of view of physical characteristics (weight, height and build) and dress and behaviour, the testers, aged between 20 and 25, were intensively trained, following the directions given in the ILO research manual (Bovenkerk, 1992). The training was provided in collaboration with either the regional employment service (in Flanders), or with private information and training centres (in Brussels and Wallonia). In addition to being instructed in the situation testing methodology, in curriculum vitae drafting techniques and in presentation skills for the contacts to be made by telephone and the face-to-face interviews, the testers were briefed on the economic sectors and occupations to be covered in the research.

Vacancies were selected from advertisements in regional and local newspapers. Unsolicited applications represented 60 per cent and 33 per cent of all usable tests in Flanders and Wallonia respectively. These proportions appear to reflect the usual behavioural pattern of jobseekers in these regions.

Presentation of the situation test findings

The findings of the ILO research are presented first for the country as a whole, then by region, economic sector, type of occupation and, finally, by type of contact with the client.

Results of the sample as a whole

During the ten months of testing, a total of 637 usable tests, that is, application procedures in which the two testers were both considered by the employer, were completed. These tests can, therefore, be used to calculate whether discrimination occurred against one of the two testers who carried out the tests in each case, that is, the representative of the majority Belgian population or the tester of Moroccan descent. The test findings are presented in table 2.1.

In the first stage of the application procedure – the initial contact by telephone (or in the case of unsolicited applications, the initial meeting with the employer) – there were 182 cases in which the testers were treated unequally. The tester of Moroccan descent was rejected 151 times, whereas the majority tester was rejected in only 31 cases. Following the research methodology, the level of net discrimination is obtained by subtracting the scores for unequal treatment for the minority applicant from those attained by the majority candidate. This results in a net discrimination against the applicant of Moroccan descent in 120 applications, or 19 per cent. In other words, in one application in five, the tester of Moroccan descent was not even given the opportunity to present his credentials.

The second stage of the procedure involves the presentation by the testers of their qualifications, resulting in either an invitation for a job interview or a rejection by the employer. Here, the total cases of unequal treatment numbered 113: the tester of Belgian origin was invited for an interview in 96 cases, whereas the tester of Moroccan descent was invited in only 17 cases. This results in a net discrimination of 79 cases during the second phase, or 12 per cent of all usable cases. After the first two stages of the application procedure, the cumulative discrimination amounted to 199 cases (120+79), or 31 per cent of the total.

The case shown on page 46 illustrates the type of discrimination the applicant of Moroccan origin faced at this stage of the application process.

In the third stage, the job interview, 25 cases (19+6) of unequal treatment were recorded. In 19 interviews, the job was offered to the tester of Belgian origin only, whereas the tester of Moroccan descent was preferred in only six cases, resulting in a net discrimination score of 13 (2 per cent of all usable cases). The second case on page 46, taken from the report form filled out by the test

Table 2.1   Results of situation tests in Belgium by region

		Total	Brussels	Flanders	Wallonia
Usable cases		637	255	181	201
First stage (telephone call)	(a) Test suspended*	154	69	9	76
	(b) Both applications accepted	301	125	117	59
	(c) Only national accepted	151	56	41	54
	(d) Only migrant accepted	31	5	14	12
Net discrimination first stage (c–d)		120	51	27	42
Net discrimination rate first stage (%)		19	20	15	21
Second stage (telephone conversation)	(a) Neither applicant invited	89	16	58	15
	(b) Both applicants invited	99	62	9	28
	(c) Only national invited	96	38	46	12
	(d) Only migrant invited	17	9	4	4
	(e) Cases pending	0	0	0	0
Net discrimination second stage (c–d)		79	29	42	8
Net discrimination rate (%)		12	11	23	4
Cumulative discrimination (stages 1+2)		199	80	69	50
Cumulative discrimination rate (%)		31	31	38	25
Third stage (job offers in interview)	(a) Both applicants invited	99	62	9	28
	(b) Interviews pending	0	0	0	0
	(c) Interviews carried out	99	62	9	28
	(d) Job not offered	37	37	0	0
	(e) Job offered to both applicants	37	10	3	24
	(f) Job offered to national only	19	11	4	4
	(g) Job offered to migrant only	6	4	2	0
Net discrimination third stage (f–g)		13	7	2	4
Net discrimination rate (%)		2	3	1	2
Cumulative discrimination (stages 1+2+3)		212	87	71	54
Cumulative discrimination rate (%)		33	34	39	27
Critical rate (%)		8	12	14	14

* Because the testers were required to turn up for an interview in another region, bring along diplomas and identity papers, or because the employers wanted to meet the testers in their homes.

supervisor, illustrates the type of "kid-glove" discrimination that tended to occur in this final phase of the application procedure. This example is of particular interest as it involved discrimination on the part of an employer who was himself of Moroccan descent.

Vacancy for a sales assistant in a fried food outlet

Applicant of Belgian origin   Telephone
The prospective employer inquired about the applicant's work experience and motivation, and then came the question of languages:

Employer: Do you speak German?
Applicant: Well, just a little – numbers . . .
Employer: But you really don't speak it? I'm sure you'll learn quickly. Come and see me tomorrow.

Applicant of Moroccan origin   Telephone
The employer started off by asking the applicant if he spoke German.

Applicant: I can count.
Employer: That's not enough, you know. You're not suitable.

Vacancy for a second-hand car salesman

Applicant of Belgian origin   Telephone
The employer invited the applicant to come for an interview the next day.
Interview
The employer, who turned out to be of Moroccan origin, described the job and the pay in a friendly way. Subsequently, he asked the tester a few questions and said, "I'll contact you soon".

Applicant of Moroccan origin   Telephone
The employer asked the applicant about his past experience and tried to discourage him: "You're not the right person for this job, you don't even know the price of a 1995 X-type car." After the tester had quoted a figure that seemed acceptable, the employer retorted: "All right...good. You can start, since you seem to be an expert."
Interview
The tester arrived for the interview and, though very strained at first, the relationship became quite cordial. The employer even addressed the tester as "son" ("Your father brought you up well, son. You're a Moroccan like me. You know about racism, how hard it is to get a job if you're a Moroccan, son.") and spoke in Moroccan dialect. The interview lasted longer than the one with the applicant of Belgian origin, and the employer seemed to suggest that the tester would be taken on . . .
"If Moroccans don't help each other, who will?"
Despite this, it was the tester of Belgian origin who was contacted the next day and offered the job.

The cumulative number of net discrimination after all three stages of the application procedure amounts to 212 cases, resulting in a net discrimination rate of 33 per cent. This means that in one-third of all the usable tests, the applicant of Belgian origin progressed further than the tester of Moroccan origin and so had more chance of getting the job. Statistically, this cumulative net discrimination rate of 33 per cent is slightly more than four times higher than the 8 per cent that represents the critical rate required to reject the null hypothesis of no discrimination at a 5 per cent significance level with a total number of usable tests of 637. It can, therefore, be concluded that significant discrimination occurs against young, semi-skilled, male applicants of Moroccan descent at the hiring stage, when compared with the treatment meted out to young applicants of Belgian origin with similar qualifications and characteristics.

At this point, unequal treatment or discrimination was considered to occur when one tester advanced a stage further in the application procedure than the other tester. If both the testers reached the same stage of the application procedure, then it was taken that they had been treated equally. Yet this does not mean that in these instances all the testers were treated in the same way. Sometimes, one of the two testers was clearly treated more favourably than the other, although the final outcome did not differ. Table 2.2 details 45 such instances, resulting in a net differential treatment that disfavours the applicant of Moroccan descent in 21 cases. If the cases of unequal treatment favouring the applicant of Belgian origin – 266 (151+96+19) – and the cases of equal but differential treatment (33) are added together, the total number of cases in which favourable treatment of the tester of Belgian origin occurred comes to 299. Unequal treatment favouring the tester of Moroccan origin occurred in 54 cases (31+17+6), and he was treated differently but favourably in 12 cases, resulting in a total number of 66 cases in which he was treated more favourably. If the total scores for the two testers are subtracted from each other, a potential maximum net discrimination rate against the Moroccan tester of 37 per cent (233 cases) is reached.

Table 2.2   Results of Belgian situation tests: treatment that is apparently equal but in reality different

Usable cases	441*
(a) Equal treatment but national favoured	33
(b) Equal treatment but migrant favoured	12
Net differential treatment (a-b)	21
Net differential treatment rate (%)	5

* Out of the total of 637 tests, only 441 (70 per cent) could be analysed

Test findings differentiated by region

Does the level of discrimination vary by geographical region? Table 2.1 also presents the test findings according to region. In all three regions, the cumulative net discrimination was considerably higher than the minimum critical rate required to reject the null hypothesis of no discrimination at a 5 per cent significance level. In Wallonia, the level of discrimination was nearly double the critical rate; in Brussels and Flanders it was nearly three times higher. There is, therefore, for all the regions strong evidence that significant discrimination against young male applicants of Moroccan descent occurs at the hiring stage. With regard to the level of discrimination, the findings indicate that this is most severe in Flanders (39 per cent), less serious in Wallonia (27 per cent), with Brussels in between the two (34 per cent). The level of discrimination in Flanders is well above the national average. In this region, nearly four in ten vacancies were closed to the young Moroccan testers because of discrimination.

The research findings from the Brussels and Wallonia regions reflect the general pattern of the total findings for all the countries studied: the incidence of discrimination is highest in the first stage of the application procedure and then diminishes with each subsequent stage. The results for the Flemish region stand out because they do not follow this pattern. Here, discrimination was found to be most severe in the second stage of the application process, when the employer was assessing whether or not to invite the tester for an interview. This implies that, when confronted with an applicant of foreign origin, the employers in Brussels and Wallonia instinctively reacted in a more discriminatory fashion than the employers in Flanders, who reacted less instantaneously. This might be due to the fact that most of the applications were of the unsolicited type, a common way of finding semi-skilled work in the Flemish region. However, Flanders nevertheless scored the highest discrimination rate of all the three regions.

Test findings differentiated by economic sector

Out of the total of 637 usable cases, the Belgian case study specifies a sectoral distribution of 609 cases. These are presented in table 2.3. The table reveals that discrimination is most severe in the hotel and catering branch of the service sector, where a net discrimination rate of 50 per cent was found. This indicates that in the hotel and catering business, one vacancy in two was closed to the applicant of foreign origin. Both the retail trade and the remainder of the service sector come in second, with a net discrimination rate of 31 per cent. Discrimination was found to be less severe in industry, which might be explained by the fact that migrants were traditionally employed in this sector.

Table 2.3   Results of Belgian situation tests by economic sector
(stages 1,2 & 3 combined)

	Retail trade	Services (remainder)	Hotel/ Catering	Industry	Other*
Usable cases	245	156	139	51	18
(a) Neither applicant invited	0	17	3	0	0
(b) Both applicants invited	127	61	49	31	13
(c) Only national invited	97	63	78	17	2
(d) Only migrant invited	21	15	9	3	3
(e) Cases pending	0	0	0	0	0
Net discrimination (c–d)	76	48	69	14	−1
Net discrimination rate (%)	31	31	50	27	−5
Critical rate (%)	13	16	17	27	46

* 28 usable cases could not be classified according to economic sector.

Statistically, the test results are valid in all branches of the service sector, where the net discrimination rates are two to three times above the required critical rate. For industry, the net discrimination rate equals the minimum score required for the findings to be statistically relevant at the 5 per cent significance level, which means that the net discrimination figure of 27 per cent should be interpreted with caution.

Test findings differentiated by type of occupation

The significance of discrimination in the hotel and catering business is confirmed when the test results are analysed by type of occupation, as presented in table 2.4. The applicant of migrant origin was rejected in 46 per cent of all the vacancies for waiters. Vacancies for sales representatives and sales assistants exhibited net discrimination rates of 36 per cent and 31 per cent respectively, which confirms the score of the retail sector as a whole (31 per cent). When applying for jobs as manual workers, the candidates of foreign origin were discriminated against in 29 per cent of the application procedures.

When analysed for statistical validity, these findings present a slightly different picture. Vacancies for waiters continue to come out on top: the net discrimination rate exceeds the critical rate by a factor of 2.7. The findings on the occurrence of discrimination in application procedures for manual workers come in second place. The net discrimination rate of 29 per cent is nearly

majority of the population are, in many instances, automatically assumed to be undocumented.

Significant discrimination was found to occur in all three regions of the country, with Flanders showing the highest rates of discrimination and Wallonia the lowest. In the former region, as many as four in ten vacancies were found to be closed to job applicants of foreign origin. Discrimination was found to be more prevalent in the service sector than in industry. This tallies with the finding that discrimination occurs especially in access to jobs that involve visual contact with clients, such as serving and selling.

Given the widespread nature of discrimination, the question raised at the beginning of this chapter as to whether the high unemployment rates of migrants can be solely attributed to the decline in industrial employment can be answered in the negative. In the process of industrial restructuring, the number of jobs in the industrial sector has, indeed, declined dramatically. However, this has been accompanied by a steep rise in employment opportunities in the service sector. As discrimination in the application procedures was found to occur mainly in this growth sector, one should not underestimate the significance of unequal treatment and outright discrimination when trying to explain the unfavourable position that migrants hold in the labour market.

Notes

[1] Based on Arrijn, Feld and Nayer (1998), with additional research and writing by Zegers de Beijl. The original report describes in full the research and the validity checks carried out in Belgium.

[2] Wrench (1996), p. 13.

[3] The 1995 annual report of the Centre for Equality of Opportunity and the Fight against Racism reported that "Moroccans" (comprising both workers of Moroccan nationality and those of Moroccan origin) made up the largest group of complainants with respect to (racial) discrimination in employment (*Centre pour l'égalité des chances et la lutte contre le racisme*, 1996, p. 22).

[4] The European Commission's 1997 survey on racism and xenophobia found that Belgium has one of the highest levels of racism in the EU. Over two-thirds of the Belgian respondents consider that their country would be better off without migrants from outside the EU. Eighty per cent said that the presence of these migrants increases unemployment levels and nearly 71 per cent of the respondents blame non-EU migrants for falling educational standards and increased insecurity (European Commission, 1998, pp. 18–28). On the occurrence of racial discrimination, harassment and violence in Belgium and the initiatives to combat them, see Spinnoy (1997).

THE OCCURRENCE OF DISCRIMINATION IN GERMANY

3

Andreas Goldberg and Dora Mourinho[1]

A net immigration country of long standing

Ever since the nineteenth century, migrant workers have been helping to fill acute labour shortages arising from the rapid expansion of German industry. Workers from Poland started coming over in the 1880s, followed by workers from Belgium, Italy and the Netherlands shortly before the First World War, then, after the Second World War, by repatriates and Germans from the newly formed German Democratic Republic. The massive, organized recruitment of foreign workers was initiated by the Government of the then Federal Republic of Germany in 1955, when a bilateral recruitment agreement was signed with the Italians. Agreements with, consecutively, Spain, Greece, Turkey, Morocco, Portugal, Tunisia and the former Socialist Federal Republic of Yugoslavia then followed suit. These workers were recruited as so-called guest workers (*Gastarbeiter*), who, after a certain period, were expected to return to their countries of origin. The principle of labour rotation was set in place to ensure that the recruitment of temporary labour did not result in permanent settlement. Although this system was soon relaxed because employers found it impractical to invest time and money in continually hiring newly arrived workers, a certain amount of rotation did take place; between 1955 and 1973 some 14 million foreigners migrated to Germany, of which 11 million later returned home. Under the rotation system, a migrant's residence status was closely linked to the individual's employment status: prolonged periods of unemployment led to residence and work permits not being renewed. Remnants of this policy, aimed at providing the labour market with foreign workers on a strictly temporary basis, continue to characterize Germany's migration policies to this day (Zegers de Beijl, 1990; Wrench, 1996; Frey and Mammey, 1996).

At the end of 1973, when the period of organized recruitment of migrant workers ceased, the foreign population in Germany stood at 4 million. Since then, as in other western European countries, the foreign population has continued to rise, mainly through families being reunited and the birth rate of migrants, as well as through the influx of large numbers of asylum seekers, both in absolute and relative terms. After the collapse of Communism in Eastern Europe in the late 1980s and early 1990s, there was also an influx of some 1.5 million ethnic Germans, referred to as resettlers, plus migrant workers under strictly enforced temporary recruitment schemes from Central and Eastern Europe. By the end of 1996, the overall foreign population had risen to 7.4 million, or roughly 8.6 per cent of the total population. About 60 per cent have been living for more than ten years in Germany, and for young people in the 15–20 age group, the majority of whom were born in the country, this proportion is as high as 70 per cent.

Turks are by far the largest single group of foreigners in Germany. With a total number of slightly over 2 million, in 1996 they made up a little under one-third of Germany's total foreign population. Nationals from the new republics of the former Socialist Federal Republic of Yugoslavia constitute the second largest group. Despite the fact that most foreigners have settled long term in Germany, only a few have been able to take up German nationality, owing to the country's restrictive naturalization rules. Until late 1998, when a centre-left government took office, the German State had not even acknowledged that it had become a *de facto* net immigration country, despite the fact that for decades now Germany has the most non-national residents in all of western Europe. The results of these policies can easily be illustrated by looking at the Turkish population. Less than a third of all Turkish immigrants has an establishment permit[2] – the most secure status – which gives migrants the right to remain in the country, even if they have been claiming social security benefits over a lengthy period of time. In 1995, 31,500 former Turkish nationals became German citizens, bringing the Turkish rate of naturalization to a mere 1.6 per cent. The residence status of most of the Turkish population as well as that of other long-term resident foreigners continues, therefore, to be fragile. At the end of the 1990s, the Government was engaged in formulating policies to make obtaining German citizenship considerably easier (Doomernik, 1998; OECD, 1998).

Migrant workers continue to be over-represented in manual and semi-skilled occupations in the manufacturing sector, especially in the steel and car manufacturing industries, in other words, in precisely the types of jobs for which they were originally recruited. Their over-representation in the service sector is due to the relatively high number of migrants doing cleaning and catering jobs. Another sector with a comparatively high rate of migrant labour is the textile industry, in which many migrant women are employed (Stalker, 1994). Although the situation of migrant workers improved slightly in the

1980s, they are still predominantly found in those sectors of the labour market where manual work is hard and/or the prospects of promotion or even the prospects for the industry as a whole are limited. This holds true for mining and energy, plus the steel, construction and textile industries (Wrench, 1996, p. 17).

Since the end of the 1970s, foreigners in Germany have been hit harder by unemployment than nationals. Whereas before then, migrants returned to their countries of origin during periods of high unemployment, following the recruitment ban and the decision of many migrants to stay in Germany and be joined by their families, their unemployment rate has been higher than that of nationals. In 1980, the overall unemployment rate of foreigners stood at 5 per cent, compared with 3.5 per cent for nationals. Since then, the difference has steadily increased. In 1994, the unemployment rate of foreigners stood at 16 per cent, that is, double the rate of nationals. The divergence was widest between younger workers, with foreigners under the age of 25 displaying an unemployment rate of 17.6 per cent, compared with 7.3 per cent for young Germans. There are also sharp differences between the various nationalities. Unemployment has hit Turks particularly badly (19.7 per cent), followed by Italians and Greeks (Frey and Mammey, 1996). As for the region in which the ILO practice tests were carried out – North Rhine-Westphalia – overall unemployment levels in 1994 stood at 11.1 per cent, but was 22 per cent for foreigners.

Whether this unfavourable position in the labour market can be explained solely by the fact that most foreigners are concentrated in industries undergoing major restructuring processes and that their educational and language abilities are below that of nationals is questionable, particularly if one remembers that the majority of young foreign people in Germany were born and educated in the country. This raises the question of the significance of discrimination against these workers when they are looking for employment. This ILO study is the first of its kind to assess the role and influence of discrimination in explaining the unfavourable labour market position of migrants in Germany.

Description of the testing procedure

Young male workers of Turkish nationality were chosen as the reference group for the situation tests. Turks represent by far the largest group of foreigners in the country and were, therefore, considered to constitute the most representative group of non-EU foreigners in Germany. The Turkish testers presented themselves as second-generation immigrants who had been born in the country and had, therefore, gone through the German education and training system. The study did not cover first-generation immigrants, since in Germany they seldom compete directly with national workers for semi-skilled jobs because of their poor command of the national language. Moreover, few unskilled applicants of any nationality would have had any prospect of success in the application procedures, given the list of requirements now being demanded by the German labour market.

The tests were carried out exclusively by telephone. Since it is customary in Germany, even in the case of jobs requiring only low skills, to present diplomas, job references and, where appropriate, other documents when applying for a job, it was not feasible to carry the testing procedure through to the third and final stage.

The tests were carried out in the region of North Rhine-Westphalia, the highly industrialized economic powerhouse of Germany's post-war economy. It was here that most foreign workers were recruited to do the sort of unskilled work that is commonly described as "three D" (dirty, dangerous and demanding). As the proportion of foreign workers in this area was still among the highest in the country when the research was carried out and as potential employers would, therefore, be used to receiving job applications from second-generation Turks, this region was the perfect choice for recreating the day-to-day experiences of young Turkish people looking for jobs at the semi-skilled level. The situation tests were conducted from November 1993 to January 1994. During the testing period, validity checks were carried out regularly, as detailed in the ILO research manual (Bovenkerk, 1992), to exclude any tester bias.

The testers were recruited from the population of university students in the city of Essen. After an initial selection had been made from the files of jobseekers at the university job placement office, a number of candidates were invited to the German project's research centre for an interview, from which two Turkish and two German male testers, aged between 20 and 25, were chosen. They had similar characteristics and were considered interchangeable. The main criteria for selection were, in addition to having an average phenotype, the ability to express themselves and to improvise and the ability to give a plausible performance as a semi-skilled jobseeker. None of them had an accent, in other words, the foreign origin of the Turkish testers was, over the telephone, apparent by name only. The testers were instructed to present themselves using nationality-specific names, in this particular case Yilmaz Oztürk (for the Turkish testers) and Stefan Niemeyer (for the German testers). The Turkish testers were instructed to present themselves in this way and to say that they had unrestricted work permits that were valid for an unlimited period of time. The four testers selected were briefed on the research project and acquainted with their roles. They were trained to respond to the wide range of questions that might come up during the telephone conversations. In order to prepare the testers for the different types of jobs for which they were to apply, job profiles and additional job-related information were obtained from the local offices of the national employment agency and job counselling centres.

Vacancies were collected from job advertisements in seven different regional newspapers; the Wednesday and Saturday editions of these newspapers contain a comprehensive selection of job offers. After the researchers had selected a number of suitable vacancies and had drawn up the corresponding applicant's profile, the testers presented themselves by telephone to the prospective employers. As there were extremely few public-sector jobs advertised, the research was limited to job applications in the private sector only.

All the telephone calls were monitored by the fieldwork supervisors. By means of a conference connection, they were able to follow the conversations and, where necessary, pass on instructions to the testers. The results and the course of the conversations were recorded on questionnaire forms, together with information about the job, the organization offering the job and details of the applicant's profile. As stipulated by the research methodology, the order in which the teams of two testers applied for a job was changed each time a new vacancy was tested.

Presentation of the situation test findings

The test findings are presented first for the region of North Rhine-Westphalia as a whole, then by economic sector, type of occupation and, finally, by size of establishment.

Results of the sample as a whole

During the three months of testing, a total of 333 vacancies were assessed, of which 175 could be used for the research. The main criterion was that the employer had to have considered, even briefly, both applicants, that is, the job had still to be available when both the testers telephoned. The findings are presented in table 3.1.

In the first stage of the application procedure – the initial contact by telephone – inequality of treatment was found to occur in 22 cases, that is, in 13 per cent of all the usable cases. Unequal treatment was confined to the Turkish applicants only: none of the applications made by the German nationals was rejected.

In 153 cases, both the testers were given the chance to present their qualifications and previous job experience during the second stage of the

Table 3.1   Results of situation tests in Germany

		Total
Usable cases		175
First stage (telephone call)	(a) Test suspended*	0
	(b) Both applications accepted	153
	(c) Only national accepted	22
	(d) Only migrant accepted	0
Net discrimination first stage (c–d)		22
Net discrimination rate first stage (%)		13
Second stage (telephone conversation)	(a) Neither applicant invited	0
	(b) Both applicants invited	142
	(c) Only national invited	11
	(d) Only migrant invited	0
	(e) Cases pending	0
Net discrimination second stage (c–d)		11
Net discrimination rate (%)		6
Cumulative discrimination (stages 1+2)		33
Cumulative discrimination rate (%)		19
Critical rate (%)		15

* Where testers were asked to travel to another region, bring diplomas or identity papers along, or where employers wanted to meet the testers in their homes.

application procedure. This resulted in 142 cases in which both the applicants were invited for an interview. Unequal treatment occurred in 11 cases, and again this only applied to the Turkish applicant. The result of the second stage is thus a net discrimination rate of 6 per cent.

The cumulative number of application procedures in which the Turkish applicant was treated unfavourably after the initial two stages of the test procedure came to 33. This results in a net cumulative discrimination rate of 19 per cent, which means that in roughly one-fifth of all the usable tests the German applicants progressed further than their Turkish counterparts and, therefore, had a better chance of getting the job. If the research had been continued into the interview stage, it is safe to assume that the net discrimination rate would have been still higher. Yet, as 19 per cent is already well above the critical rate required to reject the null hypothesis of no discrimination at a 5 per cent significance level, it can be concluded that the tests discovered significant levels of discrimination against young Turks applying for semi-skilled jobs.

The following examples illustrate the kind of unequal treatment experienced by the Turkish applicants:

**Vacancy for a job in an external service
(delivery of catalogues to private households)**

After having introduced himself, the German applicant immediately received an appointment for a job interview. Ten minutes later, the Turkish applicant telephoned. He was turned down straight away and told that the job had already been taken. Shortly afterwards, the German telephoned again using another name and was, once again, immediately invited for an interview.

Vacancy for a photographic model

The Turkish applicant called first and, after having introduced himself, he was asked to give his height. When he stated that he was 1.82m, he was turned down for being too short; he was told that the minimum height requirement (not mentioned in the job advertisement) was 1.85m. Then, the German applicant telephoned. After he gave his height (1.84m), he was invited for an interview. When he then asked whether 1.82m would still be all right, he was given a reply in the affirmative.

Vacancy for a driver's mate/production assistant

The Turkish applicant telephoned first and received a short and unfriendly answer. The employer stated that the post had already been filled and hung up abruptly. When the German candidate called, a long and detailed conversation ensued, with the employer going to great lengths to propose a suitable date and time for an interview. The meeting was later cancelled by the German tester.

Test findings differentiated by economic sector

Of the 175 usable tests, 117 were carried out in the service sector, 30 in industry and 28 in construction. The findings are presented in table 3.2.

The table shows discrimination occurring mainly in the service sector. Indeed, in the other two sectors the levels of discrimination recorded were well below the required critical rate. This means that the instances found in the industrial and construction sectors are not statistically relevant: the results may be due to chance as no convincing pattern could be established. However, for the service sector the 27 instances of unequal treatment to the detriment of the Turkish applicant represent a net discrimination rate of 23 per cent. This is well

Table 3.2   Results of German situation tests by economic sector
             (stages 1& 2 combined)

	Services	Industry	Construction
Usable cases	117	30	28
(a) Neither applicant invited	0	0	0
(b) Both applicants invited	90	26	26
(c) Only national invited	27	4	2
(d) Only migrant invited	0	0	0
(e) Cases pending	0	0	0
Net discrimination (c–d)	27	4	2
Net discrimination rate (%)	23	13	7

above the critical rate required for this finding to be statistically relevant at a
5 per cent significance level. It can, therefore, be concluded that discrimination
against Turkish job applicants is particularly prevalent in the service sector.

Test findings differentiated by type of occupation

Table 3.3 differentiates the tests findings for the service sector by type of
occupation. For 48 jobs tested involving sales activities, the Turkish applicant
was rejected in a quarter of all the applications. Of the 48 jobs in sales, 22 were
for sales representatives, the results of which are given in brackets – the Turkish
applicant was rejected in nine cases. Of the 18 tests for jobs as waiters, there was
only one case of discrimination against the Turkish applicant. When applying for
jobs as drivers, the Turkish testers were rejected in almost a quarter of the
applications, and in the remaining category of miscellaneous jobs ("Other" in the
table), comprising butcher's and baker's assistants, escorts, models, etc, almost
a third of all application procedures had to be terminated because of
discrimination against the Turkish applicant. However, none of these findings
exceeds the critical rate required to be statistically relevant at the significance
level of 5 per cent. They are, therefore, not statistically relevant and cannot be
said to provide incontrovertible proof of the occurrence of discrimination. In
other words, no statistically valid correlation between type of occupation and the
occurrence of discrimination could be established.

Test findings differentiated by size of establishment

Is the size of the establishment a reliable indicator of discrimination? This does,

Table 3.3   Results of German situation tests by type of occupation
(service sector only)

	Sales (of which sales rep.)	Waiter	Driver	Other*
Usable cases	48 (22)	18	17	34
(a) Neither applicant invited	0	0	0	0
(b) Both applicants invited	36 (13)	17	13	24
(c) Only national invited	12 (9)	1	4	10
(d) Only migrant invited	0	0	0	0
(e) Cases pending	0	0	0	0
Net discrimination (c–d)	12 (9)	1	4	10
Net discrimination rate (%)	25 (41)	6	24	29
Critical rate (%)	29 (42)	46	48	34

* This group comprises bakers, escorts, models and other casual jobs.

Table 3.4   Results of German situation tests by size of establishment

	Total	Small	Medium	Large
Usable cases	175	125	46	4
(a) Neither applicant invited	0	0	0	0
(b) Both applicants invited	142	100	38	0
(c) Only national invited	33	25	8	0
(d) Only migrant invited	0	0	0	0
(e) Cases pending	0	0	0	0
Net discrimination (c–d)	33	25	8	0
Net discrimination rate (%)	19	20	17	0
Critical rate (%)	15	18	29	98

indeed, seem to be the case, as table 3.4 shows. The tests covered 125 small enterprises, in which 25 cases of discrimination were recorded. The 46 medium-sized companies contributed a further eight to the overall total of 33 cases in which the Turkish applicant was discriminated against. In large companies, no unequal treatment was recorded. Although this is in line with the results from the other country studies indicating diminishing levels of discrimination with increasing company size, this finding should, nevertheless, be interpreted with caution, owing to the small number of tests involved. The level of discrimination uncovered in small enterprises is statistically relevant as it is higher than the required minimum critical rate. It is, therefore, safe to conclude that discrimination is more likely to occur in small enterprises than in larger ones.

Summary

The situation tests carried out in the German region of North Rhine-Westphalia provide the first concrete evidence of the extent and severity of discrimination against second-generation Turkish job applicants in Germany; it was found that one-fifth of all vacancies were closed to them because of discriminatory practices. As the research did not cover the final stage of the application procedure – the job interview – it is safe to assume that the level of discrimination is higher than that uncovered in the study.

Although discriminatory behaviour tended to be concealed, such as when an employer after hearing the applicant's Turkish name claims that the job has been filled or incorrectly claims that the Turk does not have the necessary qualifications, it can nonetheless be regarded as direct discrimination. After giving his Turkish name, the job applicant was rejected. Although no correlation could be established between discrimination and the types of jobs for which the testers applied, discrimination was found to occur at a significant level in small enterprises in the service sector. This is extremely worrying, as it is precisely in this area in which new jobs are being created (See the ILO, 1999, pp. 23–27).

To what extent can these findings be considered representative of the country as a whole? The region of North Rhine-Westphalia was chosen because of its high proportion of foreign workers. The number of migrants is far lower in the economically depressed regions of the former German Democratic Republic, yet it was notably in this area that an upsurge of racist violence occurred after German reunification in 1990 (Böhning, 1996). This indicates that the occurrence of racism and hence discrimination is not directly linked to the actual presence of foreigners,[3] and implies that the test results might well have been higher in regions with lower concentrations of foreigners. At the very least, the net discrimination rate in Germany of almost 20 per cent can be extrapolated to be applicable to the whole of the country.

As far as the first generation of migrants is concerned, it can be assumed that their high unemployment rates are due to a combination of the effects of economic restructuring and supply-side characteristics, such as a poor command of German and their age. However, supply-side deficiencies do not apply to second-generation migrants, the majority of whom were born and brought up in Germany. The research presented above provides clear evidence that the unfavourable labour market position of migrants and their disproportionately high level of unemployment (at two and a half times the rate of their German counterparts) is, to a considerable extent, attributable to the discrimination they face when they apply for jobs.

Notes

[1] Based on Goldberg and Mourinho (1996), with additional research by Zegers de Beijl. The original report describes in full the research and the validity checks carried out in Germany.

[2] *Aufenfthaltsberechtigung*, as opposed to *unbefristete Aufenthaltserlaubnis* (indefinite residence permit) and *befristete Aufenthaltserlaubnis* (residence permit of fixed duration).

[3] In 1997, 57 per cent of the German respondents in the EU-wide survey on racism and xenophobia considered their country would be better off without migrants from outside the EU. Slightly more than one in two respondents thought there were too many people from minority groups in Germany (European Commission, 1998, pp. 22–24).

THE OCCURRENCE OF DISCRIMINATION 4
IN THE NETHERLANDS

Frank Bovenkerk, Mitzi Gras, D. Ramsoedh[1]

From a *de facto* to a *de jure* net immigration country

Since the sixteenth century, the Netherlands has been a popular destination for migrants, often the victims of political suppression. Firstly, the immigrants, who would today be considered asylum seekers, consisted mainly of Huguenots fleeing religious persecution in France and Jews from eastern Europe, Portugal and Spain. Economically motivated migrants also moved to the Netherlands during its period as a major commercial power in the seventeenth century, setting up businesses, working in agriculture, as servants and even as mercenaries. In the late nineteenth century, the then booming mining industry also employed large numbers of migrant workers. Considerable proportions of all of these different groups of migrants settled permanently in the country. It was only after the Second World War that the modern-day system of organized migration got under way, resulting again in the more or less permanent settlement of large numbers of the migrants. Most came from the country's colonies or former colonies and the outlying areas of Europe. Indonesia's declaration of independence in 1945 led to an influx of ethnically Dutch, Eurasian and Moluccan immigrants, all of whom already had Dutch nationality. Following the post-war economic boom and subsequent labour shortages, migrant workers were recruited from several Mediterranean countries: bilateral recruitment agreements were concluded with Italy (1960), Spain (1961), Portugal (1963), Turkey (1964), Greece (1966), Morocco (1969), the former Socialist Federal Republic of Yugoslavia (1970) and Tunisia (1970). When the recruitment of labour was halted in 1974, migration from these countries continued in the form of family reunification.[2]

Migration from the Dutch Caribbean territory of Suriname and the Netherlands Antilles gained momentum in the years leading up to Surinamese independence in 1975. After independence, Surinamese nationals already living in the Netherlands were able to keep their Dutch citizenship, but those living in Suriname lost this right. Since then, people have been migrating from Suriname to the Netherlands largely to join family members already settled there. The late 1980s and 1990s saw an influx of highly skilled labour migrants from developed countries, involving mainly nationals from other EU Member States, Japan and the United States. This same period also saw a rise in the influx of asylum seekers, the majority of whom originated from the former Socialist Federal Republic of Yugoslavia (Zegers de Beijl, 1990).

The total number of foreigners resident in the Netherlands has been declining over the past few years. In 1997 it stood at 680,000, or 4.4 per cent of the total population, down from 5 per cent in 1993. This drop can be explained by the country's restrictive immigration policy on the one hand and a high rate of naturalization on the other. Naturalization increased considerably when the country recognized dual nationality in 1992. Foreigners can apply for naturalization after five years of residence, reduced to three years if the individual has a Dutch spouse. The naturalization rate reached almost 12 per cent in 1996, which is extremely high in comparison with other European countries, with Moroccans and Turks applying by far the most for Dutch nationality (OECD, 1998). However, since 1997, only people originating from countries that do not allow their citizens to give up their original nationality can now have dual nationality. Consequently, the naturalization rate fell again in the late 1990s (Muus, 1999).

Official recognition that the Netherlands had become a net immigration country came in 1983 when the Government formulated its so-called ethnic minorities policy. The main objective was to increase the integration and participation in Dutch society of those migrants (foreigners) and ethnic minorities (nationals) who were considered to have settled permanently in the country. Although the name and the target groups of the policy have changed over the years, its basic objective has remained the same. Currently, the policy's main target groups include people of Antillean/Aruban, Turkish, Moroccan and Surinamese descent, as well as refugees. Their overall number rose from 818,000 in 1990 to slightly over 1 million in 1998, or 6.9 per cent of the total population. People of Surinamese descent form the largest single group, followed, in descending order, by Turks, Moroccans and Antilleans/Arubans. Dutch policy papers also often refer to another category, known as the allochthonous, a group that comprises all legally resident individuals of whom at least one parent was born abroad. According to this definition, by January 1998 the allochthonous made up nearly 12 per cent of the population.[3]

The position of migrants and ethnic minorities in the labour market is poor. They are over-represented in industry, making them vulnerable to jobs losses in the current restructuring of the economy. Migrants and ethnic minorities are also over-represented in jobs at the lowest level of the service sector and in part-time and temporary work with precarious contracts. Furthermore, Turkish and Moroccan men are relatively more likely to work in agriculture and the fishing industry but are under-represented in growth sectors, such as banking and insurance. Migrant women are over-represented in industry, cleaning and catering (Wrench, 1996). Overall, some 85 per cent of all employed Turks and Moroccans work in low-wage jobs, leading Stalker (1994, p. 204) to conclude that the Dutch labour market is divided by nationality/ethnic origin, with the immigrant communities having the lowest-level jobs.

Whereas the healthy state of the Dutch economy brought unemployment rates among the Dutch majority population down to 4 per cent in 1997, the overall unemployment rate of the allochthonous population was 16 per cent, or four times that of the majority population. Although unemployment among the allochthonous population has also been declining, it has been decreasing at a slower rate than that of the majority population, resulting in an increase in the relative gap in unemployment levels between the two groups. In 1994, the unemployment rate of the allochthonous population was three times higher, 19 per cent against 6.4 per cent respectively. When these figures are broken down into specific groups, the picture becomes even more worrying. In 1997, registered employment levels among Turks stood at 31 per cent, whereas the proportion for Moroccans was 24. If one takes into account the very low labour market participation rates of both groups – 42 and 40 per cent respectively – the situation becomes even more alarming: of all Turks in the 15–24 age group, only 25 per cent are employed, while for Moroccans this proportion is only marginally higher at 29 per cent. In the 15–24 age group, young Moroccans show by far the highest unemployment rates (Muus, 1999).

Unemployment levels among the Surinamese decreased consistently during the 1990s – to 13 per cent in 1997 – with participation rates approaching those of the majority population. Interestingly, unemployment among Arubans/ Antilleans – who tend to be better educated than other migrant and minority groups – was the same rate as Moroccans, at 24 per cent. Although the Dutch Government has put numerous programmes in place to increase employment levels among the target groups of its ethnic minorities policy, the results leave much to be desired.[4] Although unemployment is going down, the relative gap between the majority population and migrants and ethnic minorities is on the rise, and this problem is compounded by the latter group's increasing over-representation among the ranks of the long-term unemployed. This situation has led to the marginalization of Turks, Moroccans and Arubans/Antilleans (Doomernik, 1998). This study on the occurrence of discrimination in access to employment in the Netherlands, the results of which are presented in the next section, reveal to what extent discrimination is contributing to their low levels of employment.

Description of the testing procedure

Young male workers of Moroccan descent were chosen as the test group. Moroccans form the third largest migrant/minority group in the Netherlands, and they were selected because they have the worst employment profile of all young people of migrant/ethnic minority origin, a situation that has barely been improving, despite the introduction of specific policy initiatives. This makes the question of the possibility of discrimination in access to employment all the more relevant. During the period of research, the Moroccan testers presented themselves as second-generation immigrants who had completed all their education in the Netherlands, were fluent in Dutch, but spoke with a slight accent.

The situation tests were carried out between December 1993 and April 1994 and covered the metropolitan, western area of the Netherlands known as the Randstad, which comprises the country's four major cities: Amsterdam, The Hague, Rotterdam and Utrecht. It is in these four cities that a large majority of the migrant and ethnic minority population is concentrated. Employers would, therefore, not be surprised to have people of Moroccan descent replying to semi-skilled job offers. As specified in the research manual (Bovenkerk, 1992), validity checks were carried out on a regular basis during the testing period to exclude any tester bias.

The testers were recruited from the population of students at the University of Utrecht. University teachers and staff from minorities' and student organizations were asked to find male Dutch and Moroccan students aged between 20 and 25 willing to participate in a study of discrimination in the labour market. Respondents were screened by telephone and those who met the job requirements were invited for an interview. A role-playing exercise, in which the would-be testers acted as jobseekers applying for a semi-skilled job, was an important element of the selection procedure. The main selection criteria were conventional appearance (average weight and height, conventional dress and hairstyle), credibility as a semi-skilled jobseeker, the ability to improvise and a manner that was neither reserved nor too forward. The Moroccan testers also had to speak Dutch fluently. Two Moroccan and two Dutch testers were selected. They resembled one other in all the objective characteristics listed above as well as in subjective qualities such as general behaviour, openness, enthusiasm and communicative abilities; they were thus considered to be interchangeable. During the research period, the pairings of the teams of testers were changed regularly, and the results screened for an eventual bias resulting from any specific combination of testers. The Moroccan testers were instructed to make themselves immediately identifiable as Moroccan over the telephone by using a typically Moroccan name (Mustafa El Mansouri) and the Dutch testers used a typically Dutch name (Jan de Wit). The Moroccans were to say that they had been born in Morocco but had come to the Netherlands when they were still very young, so that they had completed all their education in the host country.

The testers were extensively trained according to the instructions in the research manual. After the research strategy had been explained to them, they were briefed on application procedures (how to behave during an interview, what sort of questions to expect, and so on), the types of vacancies to be tested and the required level of education. Several days were spent on practical training. Mock interviews were held and videotaped, and their performance discussed afterwards. Special attention was paid to standardizing the behaviour of all the testers as much as possible; they were trained to match their responses and behaviour to different questions and in different situations. Then, after having been trained to record the test outcomes on standardized report forms, the testers each went through one real application procedure before the actual research started.

As sectors with either a very low or very high demand for labour would distort the research findings, only sectors with a steady demand for and supply of labour were included in the testing procedure. The service sector and the retail trade met these conditions best, so job vacancies were, therefore, mainly selected from these fields. Typical examples of the jobs tested in the service sector were those of waiter, bartender and kitchen/restaurant assistant in restaurants, hotels or bars, or of assistant in a cafeteria or snack bar. Among the jobs in the retail sector were those of shop assistant or salesman in grocery stores, supermarkets, bookshops as well as in shoe, flower and furniture shops. Furthermore, advertisements for working as a receptionist, driver, electrician and clerical worker were tested whenever a suitable vacancy came up.

Job vacancies were selected through newspaper advertisements. It was not possible to use commercial employment agencies, since in the Netherlands you need to prove your identity or give your fiscal number – which the fictitious applicants were not in a position to do. Random samples of advertised vacancies were drawn twice a week from a collection of national, regional and local newspapers, as well as from a list of vacancies published by the national employment agency. After the researchers had made the final selection of job offers to be tested, the applicants' job profiles were drawn up and the testers introduced themselves over the telephone to the prospective employers. Because no suitable semi-skilled job offers from public-sector employers were found, the research covered only job applications in the private sector.

The testers went twice a week to the research location to carry out the job applications by telephone under the supervision of the researchers. Prior to each test, the supervisors drew up fictitious biographies for each tester and for each job in accordance with the advertised job requirements. In order to ensure that the testers had the best possible chance of being hired, they were given all the requirements and qualifications for the job, that is, the required age and education, with two or three years of experience in a similar job. The results of the applications were recorded on standard forms, which had plenty of room for comments to be made by the testers about the way they had been treated, notably during the job interview. The testers were closely supervised by the researchers, not only during the telephone calls, but also before and after each job interview.

Presentation of the situation test findings

The test findings are presented first by region (the Randstad) and then by economic sector. It proved impossible to collect reliable information on the size of the establishments with job vacancies.

Results of the sample as a whole

During the fieldwork period, a total of 277 vacancies were selected to be tested, yielding a total of 175 usable tests, that is, 175 job applications in which both testers were able to present themselves to the prospective employer. The test findings are presented in table 4.1.

In the first stage of the procedure – the initial contact by telephone – unequal treatment between the two testers occurred in 45 cases. The Dutch candidate was given preferential treatment 43 times, the Moroccan only two times, resulting in a net discrimination rate of 23 per cent. This means that in one in four job applications, the Moroccan tester was denied the chance to proceed with the application, while the Dutch tester was able to progress to the next stage. So, even if a Moroccan applicant has outstanding qualifications and speaks fluent Dutch, he will not proceed to the next stage of the application procedure in a quarter of all applications simply because of his foreign origin.

The following example illustrates the kind of reactions obtained by the testers during the first stage:

> The Moroccan applicant called first. After he had introduced himself, he got the following response: "Sorry, but the job has already been taken." When the Dutch tester called an hour later and inquired whether the job was still available, he was immediately invited for an interview: "We haven't found anyone yet. If you're interested, come along for an interview."

In 130 cases, both the applicants were given the opportunity to put forward their qualifications and previous experience. In this second stage of the

Table 4.1   Results of situation tests in the Netherlands

		Total
Usable cases		175
First stage (telephone call)	(a) Test suspended	0
	(b) Both applications accepted	130
	(c) Only national accepted	43
	(d) Only migrant accepted	2
Net discrimination first stage (c–d)		41
Net discrimination rate first stage (%)		23
Second stage (telephone conversation)	(a) Neither applicant invited	49
	(b) Both applicants invited	48
	(c) Only national invited	17
	(d) Only migrant invited	2
	(e) Cases pending	14
Net discrimination second stage (c–d)		15
Net discrimination rate (%)		9
Cumulative discrimination (stages 1+2)		56
Cumulative discrimination rate (%)		32
Third stage (job offers in interview)	(a) Both applicants invited	48
	(b) Interviews pending	28
	(c) Interviews carried out	20
	(d) Job not offered	12
	(e) Job offered to both applicants	0
	(f) Job offered to national only	8
	(g) Job offered to migrant only	0
Net discrimination third stage (f–g)		8
Net discrimination rate (%)		5
Cumulative discrimination (stages 1+2+3)		64
Cumulative discrimination rate (%)		37
Critical rate (%)		15

application procedure, 14 cases could not be finalized during the fieldwork period and in another 49 cases neither applicant was invited for an interview, in other words, no unequal treatment occurred. Both applicants were invited for an interview in 48 cases, leaving 19 cases in which the two applicants were treated unequally. The Dutch tester was preferred in 17 cases, the Moroccan in only two. This results in a net discrimination rate of 9 per cent, bringing the cumulative discrimination rate after two stages of the application procedure to 32 per cent (23+9). The following case is typical of the type of discrimination encountered at this stage:

A meat and sausage company advertised in a newspaper for experienced help. During the telephone conversations both testers were asked their age and whether they had any experience in boning meat. Both said that they had never boned meat but that they were willing to learn. To the Dutch tester the employer said: "It's not really necessary that you're able to bone meat. You'll get on-the-job training. It's more important that you fit in with the team, and your age (20) is good. Come for an interview." The response the Moroccan tester received was: "Sorry, but it's very important that you have experience in boning meat and making sausages. We really need someone who can already do this."

Twenty applications made it successfully to the third stage – the job interview.[5] Unequal treatment occurred in eight cases, and in all of these the Dutch tester was offered the job, not the Moroccan tester. The net discrimination score of this stage came to 5 per cent, bringing the cumulative discrimination rate to 37 per cent.

In total, a cumulative net discrimination of 64 cases was found, which means that in 37 per cent of the 175 usable tests, the Dutch applicant advanced further than the Moroccan. In other words, when a young Moroccan man applies for a semi-skilled job for which an equally qualified Dutch applicant is also competing, the Dutch applicant is three times more likely to advance in the application procedure than the Moroccan. As the registered net discrimination rate is 2.5 times higher than the required critical rate, the null hypothesis of no discrimination can be rejected at a 5 per cent significance level. The conclusion can only be that discrimination against poorly educated Moroccan men occurs frequently in the Dutch labour market. This high rate of discrimination seriously affects their chances of obtaining employment. This is underlined by the test findings of the interview stage, when the Dutch candidate was offered a job 40 per cent of the time, and the Moroccan candidate received no offers.

The results of the situation tests at this point concern only blatant unequal treatment between the two testers, resulting in one tester moving on to the next stage of the application procedure, whereas the application process ends for the other tester. However, this does not imply that the testers were treated in exactly the same way in the tests where the final outcome was positive for both of them. Table 4.2 details ten cases in which the Moroccan applicant received less

Table 4.2   Results of Dutch situation tests: Treatment that is apparently equal but in reality different

Usable cases	175
(a) Equal treatment but national favoured	8
(b) Equal treatment but migrant favoured	2
Net differential treatment (a–b)	6
Net differential treatment (%)	3

favourable treatment in eight application procedures. As the Dutch applicant received less favourable treatment in two cases, the net differential treatment to the detriment of the Moroccan applicant comes to six cases, or 3 per cent. If the scores for net differential treatment and those for net discrimination after the three stages of the application procedure are added together, this makes a potential maximum discrimination score of 70 cases, or 40 per cent of the total 175 vacancies.

The following example is typical of the kind of differential treatment meted out to the Moroccan applicant:

A vacancy for a shop assistant in a men's clothing store was advertised in a local newspaper. Both testers were invited for an interview. The Moroccan tester had an interview of ten minutes, with the employer standing behind the counter. He was asked a few brief questions about his education and his former job. A few days later he was notified that he had not been selected. The Dutch tester, meanwhile, had an appointment for an interview one hour later, and was received by the employer and an assistant. The interview was held in a separate room and lasted 50 minutes. The tester was questioned in detail about his experience, and the employer provided information on the company, the various proceedings they would have to go through and the salary. The next day the Dutch tester was called and offered the job.

Test findings differentiated by economic sector

Did the level of discrimination against the Moroccan applicant differ according to economic sector? The large majority of the job vacancies tested were concentrated in the retail trade and in the hotel and catering branch of the service sector. The test findings are presented in table 4.3. The table reveals discrimination to be more severe in the retail trade, where a net discrimination

Table 4.3   Results of Dutch situation tests by economic sector*

		Retail	Hotel/ Catering
Usable cases		77	68
First stage	(a) Test suspended	0	0
(telephone call)	(b) Both applications accepted	56	49
	(c) Only national accepted	21	17
	(d) Only migrant accepted	0	2
Net discrimination first stage (c–d)		21	15
Net discrimination rate first stage (%)		27	22
Second stage	(a) Neither applicant invited	56	49
(telephone	(b) Both applicants invited	15	26
conversation)	(c) Only national invited	24	15
	(d) Only migrant invited	10	5
	(e) Cases pending	2	0
Net discrimination second stage (c–d)		14	10
Net discrimination rate (%)		18	15
Cumulative discrimination (stages 1+2)		35	25
Cumulative discrimination rate (%)		45	37
Third stage	(a) Both applicants invited	24	15
(job offers in	(b) Interviews pending	14	8
interview)	(c) Interviews carried out	10	7
	(d) Job not offered	4	5
	(e) Job offered to both applicants	0	0
	(f) Job offered to national only	6	2
	(g) Job offered to migrant only	0	0
Net discrimination third stage (f–g)		6	2
Net discrimination rate (%)		8	3
Cumulative discrimination (stages 1+2+3)		41	27
Cumulative discrimination rate (%)		53	40
Critical rate (%)		22	24

* Out of a total of 175 usable tests, 145 (83 per cent) were carried out in the retail and hotel and catering sectors. Tests in other sectors are not reported owing to the small numbers involved.

rate of 53 per cent was found. It is notable that during the first stage of the application process in which the applicant introduced himself, a higher level of direct discrimination (27 per cent) was recorded than in the overall findings

(23 per cent). In other words, nearly half the vacancies in the retail sector were closed to the Moroccan applicant. In comparison, the results for the hotel and catering sector were less severe. Here, a net discrimination rate of 40 per cent was recorded, reflecting a slightly lower than average occurrence of discrimination throughout the application process.

From a statistical point of view, the test results are valid in both sectors. The net discrimination rate found in the retail trade is 2.4 times higher than the required critical rate, whereas this figure is 1.6 for the hotel and catering sector. This means that the levels of discrimination measured in both sectors are statistically relevant at the 5 per cent significance level.

Summary

The situation tests carried out in this chapter provide clear-cut evidence that discrimination against Moroccan job applicants is widespread; one in three job openings was closed to them because of discrimination.[6] It is thus clear that discrimination against Moroccan job applicants by employers helps explain the high unemployment rates among the Moroccan population. It is safe to assume that had the tests been carried out using Turkish testers, the findings would have been the same or possibly worse, given that the overall unemployment rate of Turks is higher than that of Moroccans.

The tests covered mainly vacancies in the service sector. As this is the sector that has generated much of the growth in employment in recent years, it is not surprising that Turks and Moroccans have been far less affected by the rise in employment levels recorded in the late 1990s than the majority population.

The researchers carried out additional tests to measure the levels of discrimination against Surinamese men in gaining access to semi-skilled jobs and found the same sort of situation. In other words, the level of discrimination did not differ by ethnic group but by skills level. The ILO International Migration Paper on the Dutch situation tests (Bovenkerk, Gras and Ramsoedh, 1995) also reports on situation tests carried out with Surinamese men applying for skilled jobs. Here, the net discrimination rate recorded was substantially lower – at 18 per cent – meaning that one job in five was closed to Surinamese men because of discrimination. This would seem to indicate that the educational profile of the applicant and the skills level of the job applied for are relevant variables in predicting the level of discrimination experienced by migrant and ethnic minority applicants. This finding helps explain the differences in unemployment rates between Moroccans and Turks on the one hand and Surinamese on the other, as the latter tend to be better educated. However, education does not seem to be the sole determinant of discrimination encountered, since Arubans/Antilleans, who are generally better educated then the Surinamese, have roughly the same unemployment rates as Turks and Moroccans.

In order to assess whether gender has a bearing on differential treatment, the researchers repeated the tests with Surinamese women, at both the semi-skilled and skilled level, and with Moroccan women at the semi-skilled level. Employers' reactions to women from ethnic minorities applying for jobs were compared with the reactions encountered by Dutch women. These tests showed that, for access to semi-skilled jobs, gender is not a significant variable. The net rates of discrimination against Surinamese and Moroccan women were 36 and 35 per cent respectively, the same as the levels of discrimination against Surinamese and Moroccan men. It is only in access to skilled jobs that the rate of discrimination encountered by Surinamese women was substantially lower – at 13 per cent.[7]

On the basis of the findings of these additional tests[8] carried out with Moroccan women and Surinamese men, it can be concluded that there is a broad and undifferentiated denial of access to semi-skilled jobs for immigrants and ethnic minorities. However, neither ethnic origin nor gender proved to be relevant variables. The marginalized labour market position of migrants cannot only be attributed to low educational attainment levels or language problems, but must largely be considered to be caused by discriminatory practices on the part of employers when hiring staff.

Notes

[1] Based on Bovenkerk, Gras and Ramsoedh (1995), with additional research by Zegers de Beijl. The original report describes in full the research and the validity checks in the Netherlands.

[2] For an excellent and exhaustive overview of the rich immigration history of the Netherlands and for an examination of the various processes of settlement of various immigrant groups since the sixteenth century, see Lucassen and Penninx (1997).

[3] In Dutch parlance, both the terms "ethnic minorities" and "allochthonous" cover individuals of Dutch and foreign nationality, reflecting the fact that the country considers itself to be a net immigration country, albeit with an extremely restrictive policy with respect to new immigrants. The Dutch use an interesting mixture of definitions, including country of birth, country of birth of a person's parent(s), ethnic descent as well as nationality. For an overview of the various names and definitions used in Dutch policy papers to refer to the country's migrant and ethnic minority population, see Muus (1999).

[4] For an overview of policy initiatives to promote employment of migrant and ethnic minority workers, see Abell et al. (1997).

[5] Several interviews could not be held during the fieldwork period or were unable to be used to calculate the test results because the testers were asked to give evidence of the skills required for the job, such as boning meat, etc. In these cases, the testers brought the interview to a close.

[6] It is interesting to note that the Dutch research findings show higher levels of discrimination in access to employment than the Belgian and German results, although the general level of racism and xenophobia in the Netherlands is not only lower than in these two other countries, it is also below the EU-wide average (European Commission, 1998 pp. 22–24).

[7] This finding needs to interpreted with caution, as the total sample of application procedures tested was lower than that tested for other groups, so that the critical rate required to rule out the influence of chance could not be met. This means that the last result cannot be considered statistically significant.

[8] As similar tests were not carried out in the other countries examined in this book, the test findings have only been summarized here. For a full account of these tests, see Bovenkerk, Gras and Ramsoedh (1995).

JI5
J61
J71

THE OCCURRENCE OF DISCRIMINATION IN SPAIN 5

Colectívo IOE (Miguel Angel de Prada, Walter Actis and Carlos Pereda)[1]

A new migrant-receiving country

For centuries, Spain was a country from which large numbers of its citizens emigrated. They went, either temporarily or permanently, to its numerous colonies in the New World and elsewhere, an exodus that continued well into the twentieth century, after most of the colonies had already gained independence. The Spanish Civil War of 1936–9 led to an exodus of mostly political refugees, of whom only a few returned after democracy had been restored at the end of the 1970s.[2] Organized labour migration to other countries in western Europe started in the 1950s. Then, after more than a million Spanish workers had emigrated to other parts of western Europe, the situation turned in the early 1980s and Spain started to become a migrant-receiving country. However, not only is migration to Spain a very recent phenomenon, it is also still relatively minor. Currently, lawfully resident migrants make up just 1.3 per cent of the total population, and foreign workers account for barely 1.5 per cent of the labour force (Stalker, 1994).

There are still more Spanish citizens living abroad than there are foreigners in Spain, although the number of foreigners increased sharply in the 1990s.[3] By the end of 1996, the country's foreign population stood at 540,000, nearly half of whom are nationals from other EU countries. However, the largest single group of foreigners according to nationality are Moroccans (77,200), with the British (68,400) and Germans (45,900) in second and third place. The presence of nationals from Spain's former colonies bears out its continuing ties with those countries. The three largest groups comprise Argentinians (18,200), Peruvians (18,000) and nationals of the Dominican Republic (17,800). The overall naturalization rate stands at 1.6 per cent, the large majority of naturalized Spaniards originating from Latin America. Most EU nationals in Spain are retired and, therefore, not active in the labour market. Of a total of

162,000 foreign workers, over two-thirds originate from less developed countries. Moroccans make up by far the largest single group of foreign workers (59,200, or 36.5 per cent), followed by Peruvians (14,200) and nationals of the Dominican Republic (12,500). Apart from the latter group, most migrant workers are men. During the 1990s a considerable influx of undocumented migrants found their way into Spain's informal economy, or went to countries further north, prompting the Spanish Government to undertake several regularization campaigns (OECD, 1998; Pajares, 1998).

The large majority of both documented and undocumented migrant workers from developing countries typically carry out semi-skilled or unskilled jobs on the bottom rung of the jobs' ladder. In 1996, only 20 per cent of the labour permits granted that year went to skilled workers.[4]

Migrants are concentrated in the industrialized urban areas of Madrid and Barcelona, with smaller concentrations in the coastal areas, where migrants are mainly employed in tourism and in agriculture. During the 1980s their unemployment rates were consistently lower than those of nationals, reflecting Spain's new status as a migrant-receiving country. However, in the early 1990s foreigners started to swell the ranks of the unemployed, overtaking the unemployment rate for nationals in 1994. In 1995, the overall unemployment rate for nationals was 22.7 per cent, and for foreigners 23.1 per cent. Whereas one worker in five in other EU countries was hit by unemployment, this proportion was one in four for nationals from developing countries (Kiehl and Werner, 1998).

Description of the testing procedure

Since Moroccans make up the largest single group of foreigners in Spain, it made sense to use them as the reference group. Following the specifications laid down in the research methodology (Bovenkerk, 1992), the tests were carried out using men only, in the 20–25 age group. The tests were carried out in the provinces of Barcelona, Madrid and Málaga, as these areas are represent-ative of the geographical distribution of young Moroccan men. Because of the employment profile of the reference group, access to semi-skilled jobs was tested in the service sector in all three provinces, while the construction sector was covered in Barcelona and Madrid and the manufacturing sector in Barcelona only.[5]

Separate groups of testers were recruited in each province, reflecting regional linguistic differences on the one hand and the respective origins of the Moroccan population on the other. The Moroccan testers were recruited mainly through Moroccan associations, while the national testers were recruited through the networks of the researchers in each province. The research was carried out between September 1994 and January 1995: in Madrid work started in September and concluded in November 1994; in Barcelona the fieldwork took place between October and December 1994; in Málaga it ran from October 1994 to January 1995. In Málaga province, where access to jobs in the hotel and catering branch of the service sector was the main object of the research, it proved necessary to prolong the research period so as to take advantage of the peak hiring period of Christmas and New Year. Vacancies were selected through the job advertisements in regional and local newspapers, magazines specializing in vacancies,[6] specialized organizations such as *Fomento del Trabajo* in Barcelona and in youth information centres in all three provinces. After signing up with the national employment agency (INEM) proved ineffective, personal job advertisements in newsagents, noticeboards in supermarkets, shop windows and bars, etc, were consulted instead.

The basic criterion for selecting the testers was that they should be able to pass themselves off as semi-skilled job applicants and so have a good chance of being offered the jobs for which they had applied. The main selection criteria were conventional appearance (average height and weight, conventional dress and hairstyle), credibility as a semi-skilled jobseeker of Spanish or Moroccan origin, and the ability to improvise. Finally, the testers had to be interchangeable, so that the teams did not always have to consist of the same individuals. The testers selected were given a two-month, full-time work contract.

The teams of testers were picked independently in each of the three provinces. In Barcelona and Madrid, the candidates were auditioned until the numbers had been reduced to three pairs. Two of these pairs began doing the tests in each region, while the third remained in reserve. Since fewer tests were to be carried out in Málaga, only two pairs of testers were selected, with one carrying out the tests. In both Barcelona and Málaga it proved necessary to use one of the reserve testers: in the first case, a national, and in the second case, a Moroccan. Each area had two team supervisors, who had received special training; in Málaga one of the supervisors was a Moroccan.

The testers were given a week of intensive training, following the specifications laid out in the research manual. In the first session, a presentation was given of the ILO project, "Combating discrimination against (im)migrant workers and ethnic minorities in the world of work", and of the first stage of the application procedure. The second session was spent adapting the candidates' curriculum vitaes to fit the various semi-skilled job applications. Special attention was paid to standardizing the behaviour and the responses of all the testers.

Sessions three and four were spent looking for job vacancies and working on presentation. Both sessions were run on the basis of group dynamics.

Simulated telephone calls were made for advertised jobs. A basic script was developed for the telephone calls, which was then adapted to match each particular job vacancy. The conversations were recorded and were subsequently analysed and discussed by the candidates, the supervisors and the trainer. The training in interview techniques was worked on in the same way, and was done in the presence of the other candidates, the supervisor and the trainer, who then pointed out which aspects had been successful and which areas of presentation needed improving. In this way, each team was trained to work as a group and to follow the same procedures.

The aim of the last two sessions was to consolidate the whole process. During these sessions, the candidates and supervisors made real test calls, adjusted the curriculum vitae of the team members and selected real establishments and job vacancies to test the experiment. In order to ensure that each case or test was uniformly documented, a standardized report form was developed for each stage of the application process, and procedures for controlling the testers by the supervisors were established. During the fieldwork, validity checks were carried out by the supervisors in all three regions to exclude any tester bias.

Presentation of the situation test findings

The findings of the practice tests are presented first for the country as a whole and then by region and economic sector.

Results of the sample as a whole

During the fieldwork period, a total of 552 valid tests were carried out, that is, 552 cases in which job offers were identified and contact made by the two testers. In 167 applications, neither of the two testers was able to present their credentials, resulting in a total number of 385 cases that could be used to calculate the occurrence of discrimination in access to employment. The findings are presented in table 5.1.

During the first stage of the application procedure – the initial contact by telephone – the two testers were treated equally in 269 cases, that is, in 70 per cent of all the usable cases. Unequal treatment occurred in 116 cases. Of these, the national applicant was given preferential treatment 106 times, whereas the Moroccan applicant was preferred on only 10 occasions, resulting in a net discrimination score against the Moroccan applicant of 96 cases, or 25 per cent. In other words, in one in four applications the Moroccan applicant was not even given the opportunity to present his credentials.

Table 5.1   Results of situation tests in Spain by region

		Total	Barcelona	Madrid	Malaga
Usable cases		385	107	248	30
First stage (telephone call)	(a) Test suspended	0	0	0	0
	(b) Both applications accepted	269	48	201	20
	(c) Only national accepted	106	55	42	9
	(d) Only migrant accepted	10	4	5	1
Net discrimination first stage (c–d)		96	51	37	8
Net discrimination rate first stage (%)		25	48	15	27
Second stage (telephone conversation)	(a) Neither applicant invited	94	18	72	4
	(b) Both applicants invited	112	30	76	6
	(c) Only national invited	35	0	29	6
	(d) Only migrant invited	5	0	5	0
	(e) Cases pending	23	0	19	4
Net discrimination second stage (c–d)		30	0	24	6
Net discrimination rate (%)		8	0	10	20
Cumulative discrimination (stages 1+2)		126	51	61	14
Cumulative discrimination rate (%)		33	48	25	47
Third stage (job offers in interview)	(a) Both applicants invited	112	30	76	6
	(b) Interviews pending	61	15	41	5
	(c) Interviews carried out	51	15	35	1
	(d) Job not offered	25	8	17	0
	(e) Job offered to both applicants	9	1	8	0
	(f) Job offered to national only	14	4	9	1
	(g) Job offered to migrant only	3	2	1	0
Net discrimination third stage (f–g)		11	2	8	1
Net discrimination rate (%)		3	2	3	3
Cumulative discrimination (stages 1+2+3)		137	53	69	15
Cumulative discrimination rate (%)		36	50	28	50
Critical rate (%)		10	19	12	36

The following case illustrates the kind of direct discrimination faced by the Moroccan applicant in this first stage of the procedure:

Vacancy for an electrical technician

Spanish applicant   *Telephone*

After the Spanish tester had introduced himself, a lengthy conversation ensued in which the employer inquired about the applicant's experience. He was then invited for an interview:

Employer: So you were with XXX for four years, and you know how to mend washing machines?

Applicant: Yes. I've repaired washing machines, heaters, refrigerators, everything.

Employer: Do you have a car?

Applicant: Yes, I've got an Express.

Employer: Good. What was your name?

Applicant: My name is Salvador....

Employer: Just a moment. So, you've experience with all types of washing machines and more. Let's see, call me by ... it's more or less noon ...

Applicant: When do you want me to call by?

Employer: Let's see, come tomorrow, let's say at 10 o'clock.

Moroccan applicant   *Telephone*

When the Moroccan applicant called a few hours later, the following conversation took place:

Applicant: I'm calling about the advertisement that appeared in today's *Primerama*. My name's Mohamed.

Employer: Yes, but, you see, at the moment we only need Spanish people.

Applicant: But I have Spanish nationality.

Employer: Spanish? Yes, yes, but it's still no. The boss wouldn't let me.

The second stage of the application procedure covers all the cases in which both the testers were allowed to present their credentials, resulting in an invitation for an interview or a rejection by the employer. In 206 procedures, out of a total of 246,[7] both applicants were treated equally – they were either invited for an interview or both were rejected. Unequal treatment occurred in 40 applications. The Spanish tester only was invited for an interview in 35 cases, and the Moroccan only on five occasions, resulting in a net discrimination score of 30 cases, or 8 per cent of all usable cases. After the second stage of the application procedure had been completed, the cumulative discrimination score amounted to 126 cases (96+30), or 33 per cent of the total number of applications.

Three common types of unequal treatment occurred: (a) the Moroccan tester was told to call back later or told "we'll phone you back", whereas the Spanish tester was immediately given an appointment; (b) both the candidates were allowed to present their qualifications and job experience and both were told that they would be contacted later, but only the Spanish tester was called; and (c) both the testers were invited for an interview, but the Moroccan's appointment was cancelled or he was given a false address at which to report.

The third stage of the application procedure – the job interview – was successfully concluded in 51 cases.[8] In 34 of these, the results were similar for both the testers: in 25 cases neither was offered the job, and in nine cases both were offered the job. The Spanish applicant was preferred in 14 cases, the Moroccan in three. On the basis of these results, the net discrimination against the Moroccan applicant in this final stage was 11 cases, or 3 per cent of the total number of 385 usable test cases.

Overall, the cumulative net discrimination against the Moroccan applicant amounted to 137 cases, or 36 per cent of all the usable application procedures. This means that in more than a third of all the applications, the Spanish applicant progressed further than the Moroccan and so had more chance of getting the job. Statistically speaking, this finding represents more than three and a half times the critical rate of 10 per cent required to reject the null hypothesis of no discrimination at a significance level of 5 per cent. Significant discrimination, therefore, occurs against young, semi-skilled, Moroccan men at the hiring stage, when compared to the treatment meted out to young, semi-skilled Spanish males. This level of discrimination seriously impedes the chances of the former group of obtaining employment.

As to the issue of differential treatment, the outcome of the testing procedure was the same for both the testers, although the treatment meted out to each of them by the employers concerned was substantially different. Table 5.2 details 15 application procedures in which the Moroccan applicant received less favourable treatment 14 times and the Spanish applicant just once. This results in a net differential treatment to the detriment of the migrant applicant of 13 cases, or 3 per cent of the total number of applications tested. The ways in which the treatment of the two testers differed can be gauged by the level of interest shown by the employer to each of the testers. This manifested itself in the number and detail of the questions asked during the telephone conversations and interviews, in the degree of acceptance of references from previous employers and, in the case of the Moroccan applicant, in the querying of his legal status. If the scores for net differential treatment and those for the

Table 5.2   Results of Spanish situation tests: Treatment that is apparently equal but in reality different

Usable cases	385
(a) Equal treatment but national favoured	14
(b) Equal treatment but migrant favoured	1
Net differential treatment (a-b)	13
Net differential treatment (%)	3

cumulative net discrimination are added together, a potential maximum discrimination score of 150 cases (137+13), or 39 per cent of the total of 385 tested vacancies, results.

Test findings differentiated by region

The findings of the situation tests are also disaggregated by region in table 5.1. The total number of usable tests completed in Barcelona, Madrid and Málaga provinces were 107, 248 and 30 respectively. Although the small number of tests completed in the province of Málaga almost invalidates the statistical relevance of the test findings, it should be noted that the critical rate required to reject the null hypothesis of no discrimination was exceeded in all three provinces.

In Barcelona, where a net discrimination rate of 50 per cent was found, the critical rate established for the province was exceeded 2.6 times. In Málaga the difference between the two rates was 1.4, and in Madrid 2.2. In the provinces of Barcelona and Málaga, the cumulative discrimination rate reached 50 per cent, while it stood at 28 per cent in the province of Madrid. This means that in the former two provinces, half the vacancies tested were not open to the Moroccan applicant because of discriminatory treatment, whereas this proportion was slightly under one-third in Madrid. In other words, the levels of discrimination detected in Barcelona and Málaga were higher than the national average but lower in Madrid. In all three provinces, most of the discriminatory treatment against the Moroccan applicant occurred during the first stage of the application procedure: after the tester had introduced himself, he was immediately rejected by the employer without being given a chance to present his credentials. This type of unconcealed, direct discriminatory behaviour was found to occur far more often in Barcelona, where it generated 96 per cent of all the cases of discrimination, than in Madrid and Málaga, where the first stage generated slightly over 50 per cent of all the cases of discrimination against the Moroccan applicant. The reverse occurred in the second stage, where no additional discrimination was recorded in Barcelona, whereas roughly one-third of the total discrimination in Madrid and Málaga occurred at this point. Finally, the levels of discrimination measured during the actual job interview did not differ substantially among the provinces.

Test findings differentiated by economic sector

The test findings are differentiated by economic sector in table 5.3. This details the research findings for the hotel and catering branch of the service sector, the remainder of the service sector as well as the industrial and construction sectors. Of the total number of 385 usable tests, slightly over half were carried out in the remainder of the service sector, about a quarter in the construction sector, and the rest in manufacturing and in hotel and catering. The findings for the last two sectors should be interpreted with caution, given the low number of usable tests involved (42 and 30 completed application procedures respectively).

The results for the various sectors differ remarkably. Statistically significant levels of discrimination were recorded in industry, the service sector as well as in the hotel and catering branch of the service sector. However, this tendency was not found in construction, where the critical rate required to reject the null hypothesis of no discrimination was not exceeded. This finding might be explained by the intrinsic dynamics of this sector, which shows a higher incidence of informal employment than the others. With a cumulative net discrimination rate of 39 per cent, or three times higher than the critical rate, discrimination against Moroccan job applicants was found to be most severe in the service sector. The levels of statistical significance of discrimination in industry and in hotel and catering were similar, at 1.4 times the critical rate.

In all the sectors, the dynamics of discrimination in the application procedures followed the general trend as shown in the tests' overall findings presented in table 5.1. Most of the discriminatory behaviour against Moroccan jobseekers occurred in the first stage of the application procedure, with discrimination diminishing with each subsequent phase. Only in the industrial sector was this pattern different, with no additional discrimination taking place in the second stage and preference even being given to the Moroccan tester in one case during the job interview. However, as the total number of usable tests carried out in this sector was only 42, or 11 per cent of the total, the result should be interpreted with caution.

Characteristics of the establishments offering employment

The Spanish research report does not differentiate the research findings by size and ownership of the establishments included in the tests. However, it does

Table 5.3   Results of Spanish situation tests by economic sector

		Services (remainder)	Construction	Industry	Hotel/ Catering
Usable cases		223	90	42	30
First stage (telephone call)	(a) Test suspended	0	0	0	0
	(b) Both applications accepted	160	68	21	30
	(c) Only national accepted	60	17	20	9
	(d) Only migrant accepted	3	5	1	1
Net discrimination first stage (c–d)		57	12	19	8
Net discrimination rate first stage (%)		26	13	45	27
Second stage (telephone conversation)	(a) Neither applicant invited	48	33	9	4
	(b) Both applicants invited	72	22	12	6
	(c) Only national invited	22	7	0	6
	(d) Only migrant invited	1	4	0	0
	(e) Cases pending	17	2	0	4
Net discrimination second stage (c–d)		21	3	0	6
Net discrimination rate (%)		9	3	0	20
Cumulative discrimination (stages 1+2)		78	15	19	14
Cumulative discrimination rate (%)		35	17	45	47
Third stage (job offers in interview)	(a) Both applicants invited	72	22	12	6
	(b) Interviews pending	41	8	7	5
	(c) Interviews carried out	31	14	5	1
	(d) Job not offered	13	8	4	0
	(e) Job offered to both applicants	4	5	0	0
	(f) Job offered to national only	12	1	0	1
	(g) Job offered to migrant only	2	0	1	0
Net discrimination third stage (f–g)		10	1	−1	1
Net discrimination rate (%)		4	1	−2	3
Cumulative discrimination (stages 1+2+3)		88	16	18	15
Cumulative discrimination rate (%)		39	18	43	50
Critical rate (%)		13	21	30	36

give a breakdown by these two characteristics of the total number of tests carried out.

The majority of tests – roughly two-thirds of the total – concerned small establishments with fewer than ten employees, and virtually all were privately owned. This reflects the general employment pattern of migrant workers, who are mostly employed in small privately owned enterprises (Cachón, 1995).

Summary

These situation tests provide for the first time representative and statistically significant evidence of the occurrence of discrimination in the Spanish labour market against male Moroccan job applicants;[9] it was found that direct discrimination resulted in one in three job opportunities being closed to them. The research findings indicate that discrimination occurs mostly in the first stage of the application process, resulting in Moroccan applicants being denied the chance to present their credentials. It is, therefore, safe to assume that these findings are also applicable to other groups of immigrants from non-EU countries, whose phenotypic characteristics make them visibly different from the Spanish population (with the possible exception of emigrants from the former colonies in Latin America, in whose case the difference in phenotype and culture is less pronounced).

Significant levels of discrimination were found to occur in all the provinces covered in the research. The levels of discrimination were most pronounced in the provinces of Barcelona and Málaga, and were relatively lower in Madrid. In the former two provinces, as many as one in two application procedures resulted in the rejection of the Moroccan applicant. As the large majority of migrants live and work in these three provinces, the results can be taken to be representative of the labour market experiences of groups of visibly different migrants.

As far as the different sectors of the labour market are concerned, the occurrence of discrimination was most widespread in the hotel and catering branch of the service sector, followed by, in declining order, industry and the remainder of the service sector. The level of discrimination encountered in the construction sector was too low to be statistically relevant.

The high proportion of discrimination against young, male Moroccan migrants at the hiring stage represents a major obstacle to their chances of getting a job. Given the fact that the Moroccan testers did not demonstrate supply-side disadvantages, such as a poor command of Spanish – which most first-generation migrant workers suffer from – it is not unlikely that the real level of discrimination encountered by migrants is higher than that established in this research. Irrespective of how high the exact level of discrimination may actually be, it is clear that it contributes significantly to the unfavourable position of migrants in the Spanish labour market.

Notes

[1] Based on Colectívo IOE (1996), with additional research by Zegers de Beijl.

[2] The total number of permanent emigrants, that is, Spaniards who left the country after the Spanish Civil War and did not return, is estimated to be 300,000. Most of them moved to neighbouring France, with smaller numbers finding refuge in Argentina, Mexico and the former Soviet Union (Thomas, 1984).

[3] In 1993, an estimated 1.7 million Spanish citizens lived in other countries, of whom 45 per cent were in Europe and 53 per cent in Latin America (Stalker, 1994).

[4] As part of wider efforts to stem the influx of undocumented workers, since 1993 Spain has been operating a quota system for temporary migrants. The exact quota varies per year, but is usually around the 20,000 mark, ie about 20,000 new residence-cum-labour permits are granted every year (Pajares, 1998).

[5] As stipulated by the research methodology, access to unskilled work in the agricultural sector was not included in the research.

[6] Such as *Segunda Mano, Mercat de Treball*, etc.

[7] For 23 application procedures the second stage could not be completed during the respective fieldwork periods, that is, a definitive reply was not obtained for both the testers.

[8] Appointments for job interviews were cancelled when it was made clear that the testers would have to give proof that they had mastered the skills required for the job, when the tester was asked to travel over 100 kilometres, or when two interviews planned for one of the testers coincided.

[9] As in the Netherlands, the general level of racism and xenophobia in Spanish society was found to be among the lowest of EU Member States (European Commission 1998 p. 7; pp. 22–26). It would thus seem that openly declared racist and/or xenophobic attitudes do not appear to be a reliable indicator of the actual levels of discrimination in access to employment.

CROSS-COUNTRY ANALYSIS OF THE RESEARCH FINDINGS   6

Roger Zegers de Beijl[1]

This chapter presents a cross-country analysis of the findings of the situation tests on the occurrence of discrimination against migrant and ethnic minority workers in access to employment. It compares the respective countries' research findings as regards the occurrence of discrimination in general and its prevalence in different regions, economic sectors and types of occupations. On the basis of this analysis, conclusions are drawn as to the general nature of discrimination in everyday life.

The occurrence of discrimination

In all the countries examined, discrimination against migrant and ethnic minority job applicants was found to be widespread: it occurred sufficiently often to allow the rejection of the null hypothesis of no discrimination. The total net discrimination rates after all three stages of the application procedures had been completed were 33 per cent in Belgium, 37 per cent in the Netherlands and 36 per cent in Spain. In these three countries more than one-third of the tested vacancies for semi-skilled jobs were closed to young, male applicants of migrant and ethnic minority origin. In Germany, it proved impossible to carry out the third stage of the testing procedure. After the first two stages, the cumulative net discrimination rate was found to be 19 per cent, which is considerably lower than the results in the other three countries; it is the same as in Belgium after completion of the first stage and lower than the scores arising from the first stages in the Netherlands and Spain. The test findings are plotted on the bar chart in figure 6.1.

Discrimination was found to follow a similar pattern in all four countries covered by the research. A very large majority of direct discriminatory rejections of the migrant and ethnic minority job applicants occurred in all the countries in the first stage of the application process, resulting in these applicants being

Figure 6.1   Net discrimination by country and by stage in the application
procedure

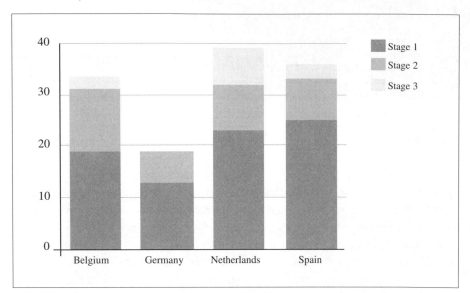

denied the opportunity to present their credentials. In other words, in the majority of the application procedures in which discrimination took place the moment the minority tester introduced himself using a foreign name typical of his origin, he was immediately rejected by the prospective employer.

The second stage of the application process, in which the testers presented their credentials and tried to obtain an invitation for a job interview, yielded significantly fewer cases of discrimination, and the third stage – the job interview – fewer still. This indicates that once migrant and ethnic minority job applicants have passed the first stage of the application procedure, their chances of being considered for the job on offer increase considerably. However, it should be remembered that, according to the calculations stipulated in the research methodology (Bovenkerk, 1992), the overall net discrimination rates recorded are likely to be only a conservative estimate of the occurrence of discriminatory treatment encountered by migrant and ethnic minority job applicants in their day-to-day lives.

Regional differences in the occurrence of discrimination

The situation tests carried out in Belgium and Spain covered different regions in those two countries. Both their findings showed variations according to region. In Belgium, discrimination in access to employment was found to occur significantly in all three regions of the country, with Flanders displaying the highest rate (39 per cent), Wallonia the lowest (27 per cent) and the Brussels region in between the two (34 per cent). The research findings from Brussels and Wallonia reflect the general pattern of all the test findings: the incidence of discrimination was highest in the first stage of the application procedure and diminished with each subsequent stage. The results for the Flemish region stand out because they do not follow this pattern. Here, discrimination was found to be most severe in the second stage, when the employer was assessing whether or not to invite the tester for an interview. This implies that, when confronted with an applicant of foreign origin, the employers in Brussels and Wallonia instinctively reacted in a more discriminatory fashion than in Flanders, where employers reacted less instantaneously. This might be due to the fact that the majority of applications in Flanders were unsolicited, which is a common way of finding semi-skilled work in the Flemish region. It should be noted, however, that Flanders nevertheless scored the highest overall discrimination rate of all three regions.

In Spain, tests were carried out in the provinces of Barcelona, Madrid and Málaga. In Barcelona and Málaga, the cumulative net discrimination rate reached 50 per cent, whereas it was 28 per cent in Madrid. This means that in the other two provinces, half the vacancies tested were not open to the Moroccan applicant because of discriminatory treatment, whereas in Madrid the proportion was slightly under one in three. In other words, the levels of discrimination detected in Barcelona and Málaga were higher than the national average, but lower in Madrid. In all three provinces, most of the discrimination against the Moroccan applicants occurred in the first stage of the application procedure, that is, after the tester had introduced himself he was immediately rejected by the employer and given no opportunity to present his credentials. This type of unconcealed, direct discriminatory behaviour was found to occur far more often in Barcelona, where it generated 96 per cent of all the cases of discrimination, than in Madrid and Málaga, where the first stage generated slightly over 50 per cent of all the cases of discrimination against the Moroccan applicants.

The occurrence of discrimination differentiated by economic sector

The distribution of job openings tested in the four countries was a function of the sectoral distribution of the migrant and ethnic minority workforce in each of the countries: sectors where migrants and ethnic minorities tended not to be employed were excluded from the research so as to reproduce as closely as possible the experiences of the respective target group when applying for a real vacancy. Focusing on sectors where migrants are represented or over-represented implies, however, that these are the sectors where they will experience relatively little discrimination in access to employment. This substantiates the statement made earlier that the research findings are probably a conservative estimate of the levels of discrimination in the labour market as a whole. At the same time, however, the sectoral distribution of the tests was influenced by the jobs on offer during the period in which the fieldwork was carried out. Access to semi-skilled jobs in the service sector and several of its branches was tested in all four countries. The industrial sector was not covered in the Netherlands, reflecting the virtually completed process of economic restructuring in this country, whereas vacancies in construction were included in Germany and Spain.

In all four countries the highest scores of discrimination against the migrant/ ethnic minority applicant occurred in the service sector and its constituent branches. The overall findings for all branches of the service sector combined are presented in table 6.1 and the rates per sector in figure 6.2. The net discrimination rates recorded in each country were clearly higher than the average, cross-sector levels of discrimination. Within the service sector, in Belgium and Spain levels of discrimination were highest in the hotel and catering sector, where half the vacancies were found to be closed to migrant and ethnic minority job applicants. In the Netherlands, this proportion was one in three. In the latter country, the migrant applicant was discriminated against in almost half the vacancies tested in the retail trade, whereas this ratio was one in three in Belgium. The remainder of the service sector scored net discrimination rates of 31 per cent and 39 per cent in Belgium and Spain respectively.

With regard to sectors in which migrant and ethnic minority workers are typically over-represented, the industrial sector in Spain had the highest net discrimination rate of all – 43 per cent. By contrast, in Belgium this sector displayed the lowest discrimination rates. Here, nearly one in three job openings was closed to the applicant of Moroccan descent. In Germany, the level of discrimination encountered in this sector was too low to be statistically relevant, which is also true of the construction sector in this country and in Spain.

It can be concluded that discrimination was found to occur in extremely high levels in the service or tertiary sector, notably in branches where contacts with clients form an essential element of the service. In the secondary or manufacturing sector, the findings differed across the countries in which access to industrial jobs was tested, whereas the levels of discrimination unearthed in the construction sector were too low to be statistically relevant.

Table 6.1   Discrimination in the service sector

	Belgium	Germany	Netherlands	Spain
Usable cases	540	117	145	253
Cumulative net discrimination	193	27	57	103
Net discrimination rate (%)	36	23	39	41
Critical rate (%)	8	18	16	12
Country-level discrimination rate (%)	33	19	37	36

Figure 6.2   Net discrimination by economic sector (only findings that met the statistical criteria)

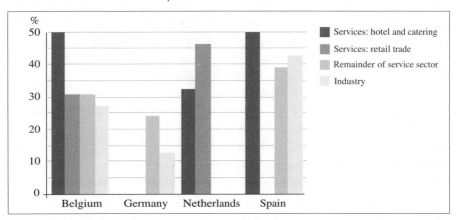

Discrimination by type of occupation

The research reports on Belgium and Germany also detail the test findings by type of occupation. In Belgium, the ethnic minority applicant found it extremely difficult to get a job as a waiter: nearly half his applications were rejected. One-third of the applications for sales representatives and assistants resulted in the minority tester being discriminated against. For jobs as a manual worker, the net discrimination rate was slightly lower – at 29 per cent.

In Germany, the differentiation of the occurrence of discrimination by type of occupation needs to be interpreted more carefully, since none of the findings was statistically relevant. However, given the fact that the results for jobs in the retail trade and jobs as sales representative were close to the required critical rate, it can be assumed that these types of jobs are particularly difficult for migrant workers to get.

These findings confirm the preponderance of discrimination against migrant and ethnic minority workers in the service sector, in particular for jobs that involve visual or direct contact with clients. As already indicated, this is a worrying finding, since it is in this sector that most new jobs are being created.

Discrimination by size of establishment and ownership

Only in the case of Germany was it possible to compile reliable information with regard to the size of the establishments offering employment. Discrimination against the migrant applicant occurred mostly in the applications for jobs in small enterprises (fewer than 50 employees). The Spanish report specifies that roughly two-thirds of all 385 vacancies tested were carried out in enterprises with fewer than ten employees. Given that the overall net discrimination rate against the migrant applicants was 36 per cent, it would not seem too unrealistic to conclude that in Spain the owners or employees of small enterprises are prone to engage in discriminatory practices.

Access to jobs in the public sector was not tested because of the formalities involved in applying for these jobs, such as the need to submit written applications and official papers (diplomas and residence permits); this would have been incompatible with the research methodology developed for testing discrimination in access to semi-skilled jobs. Moreover, not all the countries covered in this report have yet opened up public-sector employment to foreign workers.

Discussion

Discrimination against migrant and ethnic minority job applicants was found to be a phenomenon of considerable and statistical significance in all four countries in which the tests were carried out. The highest levels of discrimination were found in the Netherlands, the lowest in Germany, with Belgium and Spain in second and third place. On average, migrants were discriminated against in one in three application procedures. In interpreting these results, it should be kept in mind that, because of the rigorous nature of the research methodology, the discrimination rates uncovered can be assumed to be conservative estimates of the actual situation. The discrimination rate of one in three may, therefore, be but an indication of the scale of the problems facing migrant and ethnic minority workers in gaining employment.

The research findings show that discrimination occurs in all three stages of the recruitment process. It is at its most flagrant in the first stage, that is, when the migrant first makes contact with the employer. Blatant, direct discrimination at this point means that migrants are often not even able to present their credentials. Frequently, the migrant applicant was simply told that the vacancy had already been filled, whereas the national applicant was invited for an interview. In other instances, the migrant candidate, identified by his foreign-sounding name, was told straight away that foreigners were not wanted. In the second stage of the application procedure, discrimination occurred again when both applicants were briefly interviewed and asked to present their credentials; there were a considerable number of cases where the migrant candidate was asked for more qualifications than the native candidate, or queried about his residence status and work permits. The third stage showed that, even when the migrant candidate was offered a job, the terms and conditions of employment tended to be inferior to those offered to the national applicant. In other words, even when they were offered employment, many migrants were treated as though they were undocumented foreigners who could be easily exploited. Given the high levels of discriminatory exclusion and resulting unemployment, it would seem likely that even documented migrant workers would accept below-standard working conditions.[1]

Table 6.2 presents in detail the findings of the third stage of the application procedure – the job interview – which represents the moment when the job applicants are considered in detail by the prospective employer. In the Netherlands, none of the migrant applicants was offered a job, compared with 12 successful applications in Spain and 43 in Belgium. This means that out of all the application procedures tested, the chances of the migrant/ethnic minority applicant being offered the respective jobs were zero in the Netherlands, 3 per cent in Spain and 7 per cent in Belgium. When compared with the number of times the national applicant was offered the job in question, it is clear that both candidates did not have much chance of being successful. Since the testers' CVs had been tailor-made to meet the requirements of each job, this poor result shows how fierce competition is among young people for semi-skilled jobs. However, discrimination clearly results in further diminishing the chances of

Table 6.2   Number of job offers obtained

	Belgium	The Netherlands	Spain
Total number of jobs offered to native applicant	56	8	22
Success rate (%)	9	5	6
Total number of jobs offered to migrant applicant	43	0	12
Success rate (%)	7	0	3

migrant and ethnic minority applicants obtaining a job. These research findings provide for the first time representative and statistically reliable proof that discrimination constitutes a serious impediment to the chances of migrants finding employment in the EU.

Above average discrimination rates were detected in small privately owned enterprises in the service sector, especially for jobs that involve direct contact with clients, such as in the hotel and catering sectory and the retail trade. This is all the more troubling as it is notably in the service sector that demand for labour is relatively high and new jobs are being created. This implies that discrimination might increase in countries such as Belgium (notably in the Walloon region), Germany and Spain, where the process of economic restructuring, involving a rapid decline of employment in the secondary sector and growth in the service sector, has not yet been completed.[2] In other words, employment growth in this field will not benefit migrant workers proportionally, thus adding further to their disadvantaged position in the labour market. It is interesting to note that the average, overall levels of discrimination are virtually the same in the Netherlands and in Spain. This implies that the length of time migrants have been in a labour market does not necessary influence the treatment meted out to them by employers. In other words, discrimination does not diminish automatically over time as employers become used to the presence of migrant workers.[3]

On the basis of these cross-country findings, the following research variables were found to be related to the levels of discrimination encountered by young, male migrant and ethnic minority jobseekers when applying for semi-skilled jobs: (a) the size of the organization offering employment; (b) the economic sector; and (c) the type of occupation. With regard to the latter, occupations that involve direct contact with clients were found to be extremely difficult for migrants to obtain. The regional variation in discrimination levels found in Belgium and Spain may be explained by the different mix of sectors involved in each region. As all the regions had similar levels of concentrations of migrant and ethnic minority populations, no conclusions can be drawn as to the potential importance of this variable in other settings. The fact that the testers were taken from recently arrived or long-established migrant and ethnic minority groups had no effect on the discrimination encountered.

The research methodology of situation testing only measures the occurrence of discrimination and those variables likely to influence its manifestation. It measures the outcomes of personnel selection processes, and as such it is the only research methodology that gives an insight into the real-life experiences of jobseekers. However, the methodology cannot explain the behaviour of the decision-makers.[4] As for the high levels of discrimination in access to service-sector jobs involving contact with clients, numerous research reports indicate that the discriminatory behaviour by employers or the individuals involved in the hiring process is determined not so much by their own prejudices as by the assumed prejudices of their clients. Therefore, employing migrant and ethnic minority workers in these occupations is often considered bad for business.[5]

One of the findings that merits further examination is the high incidence of discrimination documented in the Netherlands (the highest of all the four countries examined), which, of all the countries, has the most elaborate and comprehensive anti-discrimination legislation.[6] Therefore, it follows that anti-discrimination legislation is not a guarantee that unequal treatment will not take place. Wrench provides an explanation for this finding by stating that, "as social norms become stronger against open prejudice and racist rejection, discrimination becomes more sophisticated and coded".[7] Indeed, as new social norms are laid down in legislation, they may influence the way in which discriminatory preferences are expressed, but this does necessarily mean that the final outcome will be affected. This tallies with the findings from the EU-wide representative survey in which respondents were asked to indicate their feelings on racism and xenophobia. According to the findings of this survey, the Netherlands and Spain display some of the lowest levels of racism and xenophobia, in contrast to Belgium and Germany, where racist and xenophobic sentiments are widespread (European Commission, 1998). These findings show that the way people assess themselves and the way they behave in practice do not necessarily correspond. In the case of the nationals of the Netherlands and Spain, although they don't consider themselves racist, this is not borne out by their behaviour in practice, whereas the reverse is true of Germans. It is only in the case of Belgium that attitudes and actual behaviour appear to correspond.

These research findings reveal how urgent it is to combat discrimination effectively. But how is this to be done? The next, and final, chapter provides some answers

Notes

[1] This subject, as well as other indications of discrimination during employment, is developed in Zegers de Beijl (1990).

[2] Doomernik (1998) elaborates this hypothesis further.

[3] For a discussion of the "declining discrimination hypothesis", see Becker (1957). For a refinement of Becker's hypothesis, see Friedman (1962) and Sowell (1981). For arguments against the hypothesis, see Reich (1981), Bowles (1985) and Shulman (1989)

[4] A discussion of the strengths and limitations of situation testing in comparison with other methods of measuring discrimination can be found in Chapter 2.

[5] See Wrench (1997a).

[6] See the ILO (1998) and Zegers de Beijl (1991; 1995).

[7] See Wrench (1996), p. 48.

THE WAY FORWARD: ACHIEVING EQUALITY FOR MIGRANT AND ETHNIC MINORITY WORKERS

7

Roger Zegers de Beijl[1]

In its first phase, the ILO project, "Combating discrimination against (im)migrant workers and ethnic minorities in the world of work", shows that significant and disturbing levels of discrimination are occurring in all the countries that were analysed. Overall net discrimination rates of up to 35 per cent are not uncommon, effectively meaning that at least one job vacancy in three is closed to migrant workers. By far the most flagrant discrimination occurs at the initial contact stage, when the testers attempt to present their credentials. In the course of the research it was shown that minority applicants are often simply told that a vacancy has already been filled, while national applicants are invited for an interview. This section puts forward proposals for tackling this kind of discrimination. As the findings of the second and third phases of the project have also become available, some of them have been incorporated here, too.[1]

Legislating against discrimination

Appropriate legislation can give the necessary weight to the moral, social and economic arguments against discrimination that were introduced in the introduction to this study. Comprehensive anti-discrimination legislation can send a clear signal to employers and to society as a whole that not only is discrimination morally and socially unacceptable, it also has potential costs. By outlawing discriminatory conduct in employment, the state not only informs everyone that discrimination will not be tolerated, it also encourages victims to seek redress. Thus, legislation can have both a preventative and curative effect. But in order to fulfil these roles, legislation must be adequate and enforceable. Legislation that is incomplete, vague or inaccessible is of little use.

The second phase of the ILO project comprised research to assess the scope and efficacy of anti-discrimination legislation and specific measures to combat discrimination. The countries studied were Belgium, Canada, Denmark, Finland, Germany, the Netherlands, Spain, Sweden, the United Kingdom and the United States. It was shown that, while many countries do have some form of anti-discrimination legislation in place, it is often insufficient where migrant workers are concerned and it is rarely adequately enforced. Although most of the countries studied include a specific right to equal treatment in their constitutions, in most cases the scope of the provisions does not cover differential treatment on the grounds of nationality. Furthermore, in many countries constitutional provisions cannot be directly invoked in cases of discrimination in the private sector.

With regard to the private sector, all the countries surveyed make certain discriminatory acts a criminal offence, although almost all the countries prefer discrimination in employment to come under civil law – only Belgium relies primarily on criminal law. However, substantial differences exist as to the comprehensiveness of the existing legislation. Whereas four countries – Canada, the Netherlands, the United Kingdom and the United States – can be said to have enacted relatively comprehensive anti-discrimination legislation as civil law, covering, in principle, all employment-related discrimination, other countries have only scattered provisions for dealing specifically with migrant and ethnic minority workers and then only for dealing with certain aspects of employment. In Germany and Spain, for example, discrimination in access to private-sector employment is not covered by the legislation currently in place.

To enforce existing anti-discrimination provisions, countries rely on a variety of measures. Although all the countries surveyed have bodies that deal with issues concerning migrant and ethnic minority workers, their powers vary considerably. Some have only consultative functions, such as the *Ausländerbeauftragte* in Germany, while others, such as the CRE in the United Kingdom, are fully-fledged enforcement agencies with relatively wide-ranging investigative and decision-making powers.

Countries without a powerful enforcement agency rely primarily on individual victims to press charges and thereby enforce existing legislation. Yet, the compensation available to victims of discrimination is often limited. In Germany, for instance, it is impossible for someone whose job application has been rejected on racial grounds to receive any form of compensation. In countries such as Canada, the Netherlands, the United Kingdom and the United States existing enforcement agencies fulfil important functions such as counselling affected members of the target groups, mediating between the two parties and helping victims pursue their claims before the courts.

A number of general conclusions reached from the second phase of the ILO research project shed light on the efficacy of anti-discrimination legislation and its most important elements.

Essential elements of anti-discrimination legislation[2]

The research findings of the second phase of the ILO project point to the limited utility of penal code provisions in providing redress to victims of unlawful discrimination in employment.[3] Comprehensive civil legislation appears to give victims of employment-related discrimination more chance of claiming their legal rights to equal opportunity and treatment. To facilitate their application, such legislation should not only clearly outlaw both direct and indirect discrimination, it should also contain straightforward definitions of both types of discriminatory acts. To be of relevance to non-national workers, nationality, colour, religion, race and ethnic origin should be included in the aspects of discrimination covered in such a comprehensive statute. Where not already sufficiently covered by existing legislation, other aspects – such as sex, marital status, sexual preference, political conviction, trade union membership and disability – should also be included.[4]

Since it is so difficult to prove discriminatory practices, civil anti-discrimination legislation should contain provisions to place the burden of proof on the person who is alleged to have discriminated. The accused should be required to prove that either differential treatment did not take place or, that if it did, it was not based on any prohibited grounds.

So how efficacious are these anti-discrimination statutes? The experience of several countries has shown that the mandatory monitoring and reporting by employers on the composition of their workforce according to nationality, ethnic group or minority status and under any other possible discriminatory grounds as specified in law are extremely useful tools. Requirements to adopt affirmative action programmes that actively promote the equal participation of migrants in the workplace, in addition to provisions excluding companies from acquiring government contracts for the provision of goods and services if they discriminate (contract compliance) are equally indispensable.

With regard to the crucial issue of law enforcement, the programme's findings clearly demonstrate that, in addition to the promotion of anti-discrimination legislation, having an institution that specializes in the field of equality of treatment and non-discrimination is the most effective way of guaranteeing enforcement. Such an institution should handle all individual allegations of discriminatory treatment and try to arrive at a mediated solution. To be fully effective, the institution should have wide-ranging investigatory powers. Should mediation fail, the agency should have the power to issue cease-and-desist orders aimed at obliging the alleged discriminator to stop any discriminatory practices and put equal opportunities policies in place. It should also have the power to bring cases to court. As discrimination is rarely a one-off act, provisions allowing for group complaints would enhance the impact of anti-discrimination legislation.

Training in non-discrimination[5]

Even when legislation is comprehensive and enforced, if it stands in isolation it is often still not enough to curb discrimination in employment. For a truly comprehensive anti-discrimination strategy, legislation must be supplemented by other measures, in particular by training.

In the third phase of the ILO project, training activities were assessed in six countries: Belgium, Finland, the Netherlands, Spain, the United Kingdom and the United States. Based on a methodology developed by the ILO,[6] the assessment consisted of making an inventory and then evaluating training and education activities relating to the equal treatment of migrants and ethnic minorities in the workplace. It also covered the type of training materials used and their effect on trainees. In particular, the research focused on anti-discrimination training, since this kind of training is directed at the societal majority, thus defining the problem of discrimination not as something to be resolved by migrant and ethnic minority workers but rather by its perpetrators.

The conclusions of this research show great diversity in the extent to which training is used as a tool to combat discrimination. In some countries, such as Canada, the United Kingdom and the United States, training to combat discrimination in the workplace has been developing steadily over the course of the past few decades and has been adopted by a large number of employers across the employment spectrum as a partial solution to the problem of discrimination. The Netherlands has also developed a wide variety of different training approaches that encompass a huge range of different aspects of non-discrimination and employment. In other countries, such as Belgium, Finland, Germany and Spain, progress has been much slower and less consistent. In these countries, as well as in others, much of the training that exists is directed at the migrant and ethnic minority communities, such as vocational and language training – in short, training that attempts to assist these groups to integrate more readily into mainstream society. This approach, however, deals only with supply-side disadvantages and does not take into account discrimination as a potential factor in marginalization.

The wide assortment of approaches to training that exists in these countries is remarkable. It ranges from training to change discriminatory behaviour towards migrants and ethnic minorities to training to change individuals' attitudes; from training based on information provision to training attempting to raise awareness of day-to-day discrimination; from confrontational techniques to "managing diversity" programmes. To some extent, this variety may reflect the range of anti-discrimination legislation already in place, some of which sets higher statutory obligations for employers than others.

Below are presented a number of conclusions reached from the third phase of the ILO project, namely the most effective elements of anti-discrimination training.

Essential elements of anti-discrimination training

The results of the third phase of the ILO research project[7] point to the limited use of training approaches that aim to provide information on the background to international migration and migrants' culture. The assumption behind this approach – that accurate and balanced information will automatically yield non-discriminatory behaviour – is not borne out by the evaluations. Similarly, training that aims to change people's attitudes does not appear to be effective in changing actual behaviour and has sometimes even resulted in achieving the opposite effect.

In order to achieve a change in people's behaviour in their daily contact with migrant workers, training needs to try and instil in individuals an awareness of discriminatory aspects in their own behaviour and to provide them with sufficiently concrete advice as to how to go about changing this behaviour. Training should involve information about statutory obligations with respect to equal treatment and wider governmental and company policies and it should focus on concrete exercises that are based on real-life, workplace-related situations. For this type of training to be successful in modifying the behaviour of employees throughout an organization, it is essential that all the firm's employees are trained, that the training is part of wider equal opportunities policies in the company and that these policies are actively promoted by management. More than anything, it is the training environment that needs improving.

Conclusion

The first phase of the ILO project, "Combating discrimination against (im)migrant workers and ethnic minorities in the world of work", discovered that labour market discrimination against migrants and ethnic minorities is widespread and pervasive. Over one-third of labour market opportunities are closed to minority and ethnic minority candidates. The project shows that this type of discrimination is affecting the lives of migrant and ethnic minority workers throughout the countries of western Europe. The marginalization and segregation resulting from this discrimination feed the very stereotypes and prejudices that originally generated it, to the detriment not only of the migrant and ethnic minority communities but also of society as a whole. To eradicate this discrimination is a moral and social imperative, which will also be of economic benefit to employers and, through them, to society as a whole.

The second phase of the project showed that detailed civil legislation, based on the principles embodied in international standards on equal treatment for migrant workers, is a necessary requirement if anti-discrimination strategy targeted at the world of work is to be effective. The most significant aspect of the findings is that the most positive and effective measure is the adoption of comprehensive, civil anti-discrimination legislation outlawing labour-market discrimination on the grounds of nationality, race, colour, ethnic and national origin and religion. Legislation was shown to be most effective when it outlaws both direct and indirect discrimination and provides a mandate for an independent, specialized body to enforce the provisions. Additional enforcement mechanisms, such as contract compliance, the mandatory monitoring of the labour force and target setting, are seen as complementary ways of ensuring better protection from discrimination for vulnerable groups.

Yet discrimination cannot be eliminated by legislation alone. Further measures with respect to access to jobs, promotion and training, plus training in non-discriminatory behaviour, are necessary. The third phase of the project revealed that the introduction of staff training on the subject of non-discrimination, aimed at labour-market gate-keepers[8] and other members of staff, enhances the effectiveness of the law in practice. Training aimed primarily at changing daily behaviour through providing information and courses in equality was shown to be the best way of increasing employer returns on investment in training. Most importantly, it was shown that training can only have a significant impact on workplace practices if it is part of a wider commitment on the part of the organization to eradicate discrimination, involving the visible endorsement of both upper management and the trade unions.

However, although the second and third phases of the project revealed that both legislation and training are vital components in an effective anti-discrimination strategy, they are but components. Only a combined, multi-pronged strategy aimed at tackling discrimination that is actively supported by governments and the social partners will be able to rid society totally of discrimination. Such a strategy needs to tackle discrimination from different angles, through a combination of incentives and sanctions. The experience of the countries that participated in this research project – some of which already have fairly advanced and comprehensive anti-discrimination strategies in place – has shown that particular measures can improve the lives of migrant and ethnic minority workers.

The aim of this ILO project has been to uncover the extent and level of labour-market discrimination against migrant and ethnic minority workers. It has demonstrated that such discrimination is widespread and has raised the issue of the appropriateness of legislation and training to combat this phenomenon. The findings that have emerged from the project, and which will be reflected in further ILO activities, will hopefully inspire as well as guide governments, employers, trade unions and pressure groups throughout Europe and elsewhere in the world to greater efforts. It is hoped that these findings will countries to adopt comprehensive, multi-faceted measures to help eradicate the discrimination that migrants and ethnic minorities face on a daily basis.

Notes

[1] This section is taken from the ILO (1998).

[2] This section is taken from Zegers de Beijl (1997).

[3] See Zegers de Beijl (1991), Rutherglen (1994), Ventura (1995), Goldberg, Mourinho and Kulke (1996), Colectívo IOE and Pérez Molina (1996), Vuori (1996), Hansen and McClure (1998), Arrijn, Feld and Nayer (1998).

[4] Mention should be made here of the proposals by the ILO's Committee of Experts on the Application of Conventions and Recommendations to widen the scope of Convention No. 111 by including the following criteria: age, disability, family responsibilities, language, matrimonial status, nationality, property, sexual orientation, state of health and trade union affiliation. See the ILO (1996).

[5] This section is taken from the ILO (1998).

[6] See Wrench and Taylor (1993).

[7] See Colectívo IOE (1996); Castelain-Kinet et al. (1998); Taylor, Powell and Wrench (1997).

[8] By "gate-keeper" is meant all job-centre staff, personnel department representatives, line managers and other players that mediate between the employer and potential employee in the hiring process.

BIBLIOGRAPHY

Abell, J. P.; Havelaar, A. E.; Dankoor, M. M. 1997. *The documentation and evaluation of anti-discrimination training activities in the Netherlands*, International Migration Paper No. 16. Geneva, ILO.

Arrijn, P.; Feld, S.; Nayer, A. 1998. *Discrimination in access to employment on grounds of foreign origin: The case of Belgium*, International Migration Paper No. 23E. Geneva, ILO.

Banton, M. 1994. *Discrimination*. London, Open University Press.

—. 1997. "The ethics of practice testing", in *New Community*, (23) 3, pp. 413–420.

—; Harwood, J. 1975. *The race concept*. Newton Abbot (United Kingdom), David & Charles Publishers.

Bataille, P. 1977. *Le racisme au travail*. Paris, La Découverte.

Becker, G. 1957. *The economics of discrimination*. Chicago, The University of Chicago Press.

—; Sowell, T.; Vonnegut Jr., K. 1981. *Discrimination, affirmative action and equal opportunity*. Vancouver, Fraser Institute.

Bendick Jr., M. 1989. *Auditing race discrimination in hiring: A research design*. Washington, DC, Bendick and Egan Economic Consultants Inc.

—. 1996. *Discrimination against racial/ethnic minorities in access to employment in the United States: Empirical findings from situation testing*, International Migration Paper No. 12. Geneva, ILO.

—; Jackson, C.; Reinoso, V.; Hodges, L. 1991. "Discrimination against Latino job applicants. A controlled experiment", in *Human Resource Management*, 30 (4), pp. 469–84.

—; Jackson, C.; Reinoso, V. 1993. *Measuring employment discrimination through controlled experiments*. Washington, DC, Fair Employment Council of Greater Washington.

Blalock, H. M. 1972. *Social statistics*. London, McGraw-Hill.

Böhning, W. R. 1995. "Top end and bottom end labour import in the United States and Europe: Historical evolution and sustainability", in Böhning, W. R.; Zegers de Beijl, R.: *The integration of migrant workers in the labour market: Policies and their impact.* Geneva, ILO.

—. 1996. *Melting pot or salad bowl – Socio-economic integration matters most!,* Paper presented at the Migration Dialogue Meeting on Immigration Issues and Integration Policy, Chicago, 25–28 April.

Bovenkerk, F. 1992. *Testing discrimination in natural experiments: A manual for international comparative research on discrimination on the grounds of "race" and ethnic origin.* Geneva, ILO.

—; Breuning-van Leeuwen, E. 1978. "Rasdiscriminatie en rasvooroordeel op de Amsterdamse arbeidsmarkt", in Bovenkerk, F. (ed.): *Omdat zij anders zijn: Patronen van rasdiscriminatie in Nederland.* Meppel, Boom.

—; Kilborne, B.; Raveau, F.; Smith, D. 1979. "Comparative Aspects of Research on Discrimination Against Non-White Citizens in Great Britain, France and the Netherlands", in Berting, J.; Jurkovich, R.: *Problems in International Comparative research in the Social Sciences.* Oxford, Pergamon Press.

—; Gras, M. J. I.; Ramsoedh, D. (with the assistance of Dankoor, M.; Havelaar, M.). 1995. *Discrimination against migrant workers and ethnic minorities in access to employment in the Netherlands,* International Migration Paper No. 4. Geneva, ILO.

Bowles, S. 1985. "The production process in a competitive economy: Walrasian, neo-Hobbesian and Marxian models", in *American Economic Review,* 75 (3), pp. 16–36.

Brown, C.; Gay, P. 1985. *Racial discrimination: 17 years after the Act.* London, Policy Studies Institute.

Büyükbozkoyum, O.; Stamatiou, M.; Stolk, M. 1991. "Turkse HTS'ers zoeken werk: verslag van een sollicitatie experiment", in *Sociologische Gids,* XXXVIII (3), pp. 197–192.

Cachón, L. 1995. *Preventing racism at the workplace. Report on Spain.* Dublin, European Foundation for the Improvement of Living and Working Conditions.

Castelain-Kinet, F.; Bouquin, S.; Delagrange, H.; Denutte, T. 1998. *Pratique de formation antidiscriminatoires en Belgique,* International Migration Paper No. 22. Geneva, ILO.

Centre pour l'égalité des chances et la lutte contre le racisme. 1996. *Rapport annuel 1995.* Brussels.

Colectívo IOE. 1996. "Discrimination against Moroccan workers in access to employment", in Colectívo IOE and Pérez Molina, R.: *Labour market discrimination against migrant workers in Spain,* International Migration Paper, No. 9. Geneva, ILO.

Commission Nationale Consultative des Droits de l'Homme (CNCDH). 1996. *La lutte contre le racisme et la xénophobie: Exclusion et droits de l'homme*. Paris.

—. 1998. *La lutte contre le racisme et la xénophobie: Exclusion et droits de l'homme*. Paris.

Commission for Racial Equality (CRE). 1995. *Racial equality means business: A standard for racial equality for employers*. London.

Cross, H.; Kenney, G.; Mell, J.; Zimmermann, W. 1990. *Employer hiring practices: Differential treatment of Hispanic and Anglo job seekers*. Washington DC, The Urban Institute Press.

Daniel, W. W. 1968. *Racial discrimination in England*. Harmondsworth, Penguin Books.

Darity Jr., W. 1995. *Economics and discrimination*. Aldershot, Edward Elgar Publishers.

De Rudder, V.; Tripier, M.; Vourc'h, F. 1995. *La prévention du racisme dans l'entreprise en France*. Dublin, European Foundation for the Improvement of Living and Working Conditions.

Den Uyl, R.; Choenni, C.; Bovenkerk, F. 1986. *Mag het ook een buitenlander wezen? Discriminatie bij uitzendbureaus*. Utrecht, Landelijk Bureau Racismebestrijding.

Deutscher, I. 1973. *What we say/What we do: Sentiments and acts*. Glenview (Illinois), Scott, Foresman and Cy.

Dex, S. 1992. *The costs of discriminating against migrant workers: An international review*. Geneva, ILO.

Doomernik, J. 1998. *The effectiveness of integration policies towards immigrants and their descendants in France, Germany and the Netherlands*. Geneva, ILO.

Edwards, J. 1995. *When race counts: The morality of racial preference in Britain and America*. New York, Routledge.

Esmail, A; Everington, S. 1993. "Racial discrimination against doctors from ethnic minorities", in *British Medical Journal*, 306, pp. 691–692.

Essed, P. 1991. *Everyday racism*. London, Sage Publishers.

European Commission. 1998. *Racism and xenophobia in Europe*. Luxembourg, Office for Official Publications of the European Communities.

Fassman, H.; Münz, R. 1992. "Patterns and trends of international migration in western Europe", in *Population and Development Review*, 18 (3), pp. 457–480.

Fix, M.; Struyk, R. 1993. *Clear and convincing evidence: Measurement of discrimination in America*. Washington, DC, The Urban Institute Press.

—; Galster, G.; Struyk, R. 1993. "An overview of auditing for discrimination", in Fix, M.; Struyk, R.: *Clear and convincing evidence: Measurement of discrimination in America*. Washington DC, The Urban Institute Press.

Frey, M.; Mammey, U. 1996. *Impact of migration in the receiving countries: Germany*. Geneva, International Organization for Migration (IOM).

Friedman, M. 1962. *Capitalism and freedom*. Chicago, University of Chicago Press.

Goldberg, A.; Mourinho, D. 1996. "Empirical proof of discrimination against foreign workers in labour market access: Report of experience in Germany", in Goldberg, A.; Mourinho, D.; Kulke, U.: *Labour market discrimination against foreign workers in Germany*, International Migration Paper No. 7. Geneva, ILO.

Griffin, J. H. 1960. *Black like me.* New York, Signet Books.

Groenendijk, K.; Hampsink, R. 1995. *Temporary employment of migrants in Europe.* Nijmegen, Katholieke Universiteit.

Hansen, N. E.; McClure, I. 1998. *Protecting migrants and ethnic minorities from discrimination in employment: The Danish experience*, International Migration Paper No. 25. Geneva, ILO.

Henry, F. 1989. *Who gets the work in 1989?* Ottawa, Economic Council of Canada.

—; Ginzberg, E. 1985. *Who gets the work? A test of racial discrimination in employment.* Toronto, Social Planning Council of Metropolitan Toronto, jointly with the Urban Alliance on Race Relations.

Hoffmann-Nowotny, H. J. 1976. *European migrations after the Second World War,* Paper presented to the Conference on Migration, New Harmony (Indiana), April 14.

Hubbock, J.; Carter, S. 1980. *Half a chance?* London, Commission for Racial Equality (CRE).

International Labour Organization (ILO). 1996. *Equality in employment and occupation: International Labour Conference, 83rd session, 1996.* Special survey on equality in employment and occupation in respect of Convention No. 111; Report of the Committee of Experts on the Application of Conventions and Recommendations. Geneva.

—. 1997. *Protecting the most vulnerable of today's workers,* Discussion Paper for the Tripartite Meeting of Experts on Future ILO Activities in the Field of Migration. Geneva.

—. 1998. *A draft manual on achieving equality for migrant and ethnic minority workers.* Geneva.

—. 1999. *Decent work*, Report of the Director-General to the International Labour Conference, 87th session. Geneva.

Jenkins, R. 1986. *Racism and recruitment: Managers, organizations and equal opportunity in the labour market.* Cambridge, Cambridge University Press.

Kiehl, M.; Werner, H. 1998. *The labour market situation of EU and of third country nationals in the European Union.* Nuremberg, Institut für Arbeitsmarkt- und Berufsforschung der Bundesanstalt für Arbeit.

Kirschenman, J.; Neckerman, K. M. 1991. "We'd love to hire them but...", in Jencks, C.; Peterson, P.E.: *The urban underclass*. Washington DC, The Brookings Institution.

La Pierre, R. T. 1934. "Attitudes vs. actions", in *Social Forces*, 13, pp. 230–237.

Lim, L. 1996. *More and better jobs for women: An action guide*. Geneva, ILO.

Lindburg, L. (in consultation with Niessen, J.). 1998. *Plus sum gain: Business investment in the socio-economic inclusion of Europe's immigrant and ethnic minority communities*. Brussels, Migration Policy Group.

Lucassen, L.; Penninx, R. 1997. *Newcomers: Immigrants and their descendants in the Netherlands 1550–1995*. Amsterdam, Het Spinhuis.

McIntosh, N.; Smith, D. 1974. "The extent of racial discrimination", in *Political and Economic Planning Broadsheet*, 547.

Meloen, J. D. 1991. *Makkelijker gezegd... een onderzoek naar de werking van een gedragscode voor uitzendbureaus ter voorkoming van discriminatie*. The Hague, Ministerie van Sociale Zaken.

Muus, P. J. 1999. *Migration, immigrants and policy in the Netherlands* (1998 SOPEMI report on the Netherlands). Utrecht, European Research Centre on Migration and Ethnic Relations.

Newman, J. 1978. "Discrimination in recruitment: An empirical analysis", in *Industrial and Labour Relations Review*, 32 (1), pp. 15–23.

Newman, J. M.; Krzystofiak, F. 1979. "Self-report versus unobtrusive measures: Balancing method variance and ethical concerns in employment discrimination research", in *Journal of Applied Psychology*, 64 (1), pp. 82–85.

Organisation for Economic Co-operation and Development (OECD). 1998. *Trends in international migration*. Paris.

Pajares, M. 1998. *La inmigración en España: Retos y propuestas*. Barcelona, Icaria Editorial.

Raskin, C. 1993. *De facto discrimination, immigrant workers and ethnic minorities: A Canadian overview*. Geneva, ILO.

Reich, M. 1981. *Racial inequality*. Princeton, Princeton University Press.

Reynolds, P. D. 1979. *Ethical dilemmas and social science research*. San Francisco, Jossey Bass Publishers.

Riach, P. A.; Rich, J. 1992. "Measuring discrimination by direct experimental methods", in *Journal of Post Keynesian Economics*, 14 (2), pp. 134–150.

Rist, R. C. 1978. *Guest workers in Germany: The prospects for pluralism*. New York, Praeger Publishers.

Rutherglen, G. 1994. *Protecting aliens, immigrants and ethnic minorities from discrimination in employment: The experience in the United States*. Geneva, ILO.

Shulman, S. 1989. "A critique of the declining discrimination hypothesis", in Shulman, S.; Darity, W. (eds.): *The question of discrimination: Racial inequality in the US labor market.* Middletown, Wesleyan University Press.

Simpson, A.; Stevenson, J. 1994. *Half a chance, still?* Nottingham, Racial Equality Council.

Sowell, T. 1981. *Markets and minorities.* New York, Basic Books.

Spinnoy, P. 1997. "Movement against racism, anti-semitism and xenophobia (Belgium): History and development", in Oakly, R.: *Tackling racist and xenophobic violence in Europe: Case studies.* Strasbourg, Council of Europe.

Stalker, P. 1994. *The work of strangers.* Geneva, ILO.

—. 2000. *Workers without frontiers: The impact of globalization on international migration,* Geneva, ILO, and Boulder (Colorado), Lynne Rienner.

Taylor, P.; Powell, P.; Wrench, J. 1997. *The evaluation of anti-discrimination training activities in the United Kingdom,* International Migration Paper No. 21. Geneva, ILO.

Thomas, H. 1984. *The Spanish Civil War.* Harmondsworth, Penguin Books.

Turner, M.; Fix, M.; Struyk, R. 1991. *Opportunities denied, opportunities diminished: Discrimination in hiring.* Washington DC, The Urban Institute Press.

United States General Accounting Office (GAO). 1992. *Nonimmigrant alien workers in the US labor market,* Report to the Chairman, Subcommittee on immigration and refugee affairs, Committee on the Judiciary, US Senate, April.

Ventura, C. 1995. *From outlawing discrimination to promoting equality: Canada's experience with anti-discrimination legislation,* International Migration Paper No. 6. Geneva, ILO.

Vuori, K. 1997. *Anti-discrimination training activities in Finland,* International Migration Paper No. 18. Geneva, ILO.

—; (with the assistance of Zegers de Beijl, R.). 1996. *Protecting (im)migrants and ethnic minorities from discrimination in employment: Finnish and Swedish experiences,* International Migration Paper No. 14. Geneva, ILO.

Wallraff, G. 1985. *Ganz unten.* Berlin, Kiepenheuer und Witz.

—. 1988. *Lowest of the low* (translation). London, Methuen.

Wrench, J. 1996. *Preventing racism at the workplace: A report on 16 European countries.* Luxembourg, Office for Official Publications of the European Communities.

—. 1997a. "The mechanisms of exclusion: Ethnic minorities and labour markets", in *Nordic Labour Journal,* 1.

—. 1997b. *European compendium of good practice for the prevention of racism at the workplace.* Dublin, European Foundation for the Improvement of Living and Working Conditions.

—; Taylor, P. 1993. *Research manual on the evaluation of anti-discrimination training activities.* Geneva, ILO.

Zegers de Beijl, R. 1990. *Discrimination of migrant workers in Western Europe.* Geneva, ILO.

—. 1991. *Although equal before the law... The scope of anti-discrimination legislation and its effects on labour market discrimination against migrant workers in the United Kingdom, the Netherlands and Sweden.* Geneva, ILO.

—. 1995. "Labour market integration and legislative measures to combat discrimination against migrant workers", in Böhning, W. R.; Zegers de Beijl, R.: *The integration of migrant workers in the labour market: Policies and their impact.* Geneva, ILO.

—. 1997. *Combating discrimination against migrant workers: international standards, national legislation and voluntary measures – the need for a multi-pronged strategy,* Paper presented to the Seminar on Immigration, Racism and Racial Discrimination of the United Nations Centre for Human Rights, Geneva, 5–9 May.

Books on migration and employment

Workers without frontiers
The impact of globalization on international migration

Peter Stalker

This unique assessment of a complex and contentious issue brings together the latest information on international migration in the context of a global economy. Redressing a gap in most discussions of globalization, Stalker examines how migration interacts with movements of goods and capital, and how it is closely tied to social and economic changes. Will globalization lead to economic convergence that will eventually cause migration pressures to subside, or will the years of upheaval that lie ahead release new migrant flows?

ISBN 92-2-111383-3 (hardcover)   168 pages   2000   60 Swiss francs
ISBN 92-2 110854-6 (softcover)   168 pages   2000   30 Swiss francs

Books on migration and employment

The work of strangers
A survey of international labour migration

Peter Stalker

The migration of workers across international boundaries is one of the most striking aspects of the globalization of the world economy, with a major impact on well over 100 countries. This important study provides a lively analysis of economic migration spanning the globe. The author brings together a vast amount of evidence on the many issues raised by labour migration – its volume, characteristic effects, the reactions it provokes and the policies it requires. The book first paints an overall picture, and then examines the recent experience of some 20 countries and several regions.

There are numerous charts and statistical tables, including a comprehensive "global economic migration table".

ISBN 92-2-108521-X   320 pages   1994   45 Swiss francs

Books on migration and employment

Employing foreign workers
A manual on policies and procedures of special interest to middle- and low-income countries

W.R.Böhning

This manual sets out the considerations and options that policy makers and academics can draw upon when they are faced with questions on migrant workers, such as the involvement of employers' and workers' organizations, the irregular inflow of workers, illegal employment, and whom to admit and under what conditions. The book will be especially useful in countries confronted for the first time with the employment of foreigners.

"... useful to researchers and those interested in practical guidelines for thinking about labor migration. Roger Böhning is the world's most knowledgeable international civil servant who deals with migration. The strength of this book is that it lays out the basic questions in the order that a policymaker charged with 'doing something' about labour migration would confront them."

International Migration Review, Spring 1998

ISBN 92-2-109453-7   100 pages   1996   20 Swiss francs

Books on migration and employment

Sending workers abroad
A manual for low- and middle-income countries

Manolo Abella

This book examines the roles played by the state and the private sector in organizing labour migration. It draws on international experience to illustrate the many elements and practical measures that make up a programme for sending workers abroad, and suggests principles and concepts that could be used to reconcile some of the inherent conflicts among policy goals. The author explores whether and how migrant workers should be controlled and regulated to safeguard the interests of the sending state without infringing basic individual rights.

"... a must for policy-makers who are involved in foreign employment. Its usefulness can also be extended to those who are involved at the operational level, such as policy-makers, recruitment agencies (both public and private), welfare support groups, etc. It is also useful reading for students wanting to know more about the labour-market institutions of foreign employment in various developing countries."

ASEAN Economic Bulletin, August 1998

ISBN 92-2-108525-2   120 pages   1997   20 Swiss francs

Books on migration and employment

Affirmative action in the employment of ethnic minorities and persons with disabilities

Jane Hodges-Aeberhard and Carl Raskin

Using the insights of eight national case studies, this book examines current trends in the implementation of affirmative action in employment for ethnic minorities and persons with disabilities. It analyses how legislative enactment, general policy measures and voluntary programmes have been tailored to particular national circumstances, and describes the policy implications of the successes and pitfalls of the activities highlighted in the case studies.

"The book is a useful resource for those involved with affirmative action, legislators world-wide, and all people interested in making this world a better place to live for everyone including the marginalized. The aims of the International Labour Organization should be given support and promoted."

International Third World Studies Journal and Review,
Volume 9, 1997

ISBN 92-2-109521-5   120 pages   1997   20 Swiss francs